MW00711586

All Eyes Up Here!

A PORTRAIT OF EFFECTIVE TEACHING

BY

DR. TEE CARR

Written with humor and humanity, Dr. Carr's stories of
teachers and children will make you laugh, cry, and — think!

CARR
ENTERPRISES

We wish to acknowledge the following publishers and individuals for granting permission to reprint the following material:

Excerpt from *Teacher and Child* by Dr. Haim G. Ginott, (1973). Published by Collier Books (Quality Paperbacks, 1993). Reprinted by permission of Dr. Alice Ginott.

Excerpt from *In Search of Excellence: Lessons from America's Best Run Companies.* Published by HarperCollins Publishers, Inc. © 1982 by Thomas J. Peters and Robert H. Waterman, Jr. Reprinted by permission of HarperCollins.

Excerpt from *Sweaty Palms: The Neglected Art of Being Interviewed* by H. Anthony Medley. © 1978. Reprinted by permission of Von Nostrond, Reinhold, New York.

Permission granted by Peabody Hotel Group for use of their registered trademarks in the poem, "I Want To Come Back as A Peabody Duck."

(Continued on Page 274)

Copyright © 1996 by Dr. Tee Carr
All rights reserved. No portion of this book may be reproduced or utilized in any form, or by any electronic, mechanical, or other means, including photocopying, recording, or by any information storage and retrieval system, without the prior written permission of the publisher.

Printed in the United States of America

First edition published in 1996
Second edition published in 1999

Library of Congress Catalog Card Number 96-069458
  Carr, Dr. Tee
     All Eyes Up Here! A Portrait of Effective Teaching: for prospective
     and experienced teachers, administrators, parents, and everyone
     who cares about the future of our children; takes you into schools
     and classrooms to see the good things happening there; draws
     upon practical experiences of classroom teachers and principals.
     Second edition. Includes index.
ISBN 1-892897-02-4 $14.95

Cover and illustrations by Sherry Hulgan
Cover layout by Graphic Advertising

Attention: Schools and Corporations
Books are available at volume discounts for schools or organizations. Purchase Orders welcome. Please contact:

CARR Enterprises
3 Belvoir Circle
Chattanooga, TN 37412
Office: 423-698-5685
Fax: 423-698-3182

A Book About Teaching That You Can't Put Down!

"A thoughtful, touching book that embraces the art and science of teaching. It should be on every educator's desk!"

Lu Lewis
Southeastern Teacher of the Year

"'All Eyes Up Here!' reaffirms the reason I'm in education. I wish I had had this book 20 years ago when I started teaching. Although I was excited, this would have shown me the real reason for teaching— having a love for children and a desire to learn."

Mary Anderson
Tennessee elementary principal

"Too often in today's world, teaching has become a mechanical task. Drilling, testing, and dispensing information are frequently the tools of the trade. But there is a deeper, more sacred side of teaching. A teacher, through a smile or a pat on the back, can change the direction of a young person's life. That is the heart and soul of teaching—making a real difference. That is what Dr. Tee Carr captures in this book."

Dr. Terrence E. Deal
Professor of Educational Leadership, Vanderbilt
Co-author of *Corporate Cultures* and *Leading With Soul*

"Anyone who has a child in a classroom will find this book enjoyable and entertaining. Parents, expecially, will find it a resource that will benefit them when volunteering in the classroom. Tee's book is a celebration of success and of the goodness of teaching."

Dr. Margaret Smith
Director, Student Teaching Program
The University of Tennessee at Chattanooga

iii

"'All Eyes Up Here!' is an important tool for new and experienced teachers. Dr. Carr has included insights on the basics of classroom management, the school environment, stress relief, and human dignity in a wonderful book that is written in a supportive way by one who is passionate and knowledgeable about what is important in teaching. Keep this book where you can reach it!"

Monty Coggins
North Carolina "Teacher of The Year"

"'All Eyes Up Here! A Portrait of Effective Teaching' is Tee Carr's recipe for successful teaching. She blends one lifetime of teaching excellence with a measure of practicality laced with just a hint of theory. Fold in a rich mix of motivation and inspiration. Top with a dollop of humor and pride in the profession. Serve to hungry beginning teachers or as a nostalgic dish to veteran teachers who have forgotten the pleasure of teaching. For all of us in education, Tee provides us a feast filled with wisdom and no calories."

Dr. Dick Abrahamson, Professor of Literature
for Children and Young Adults, The University of Houston
Author of "To Beth's First-Grade Teacher"

"If I had read Tee Carr's 'All Eyes Up Here!' when I started teaching many years ago, it would have made a major difference in my first-day mindset. I would have walked into that classroom with deep pride in being a teacher, the excitement of knowing I might be the one to make a sparkling difference in the lives of my children, and a briefcase loaded with great ideas to get me started.

'All Eyes Up Here!' should be read by beginning teachers who want to make sure they get started with creativity and confidence . . . by experienced teachers who feel the need for a spiritual battery charge . . . by administrators who live in daily danger of forgetting where the real action is . . . and by parents who want to see into the heart and mind of a real teacher in order to become a better partner in the development of their children."

Dalton Roberts
Columnist, *The Chattanooga Times*

iv

CONTENTS

Books by Dr. Tee Carr

All Eyes Up Here!
A Portrait of Effective Teaching

**How Come The Wise Men
Are In The
DEMPSTER DUMPSTER®?**
A Celebration of Children

To Mama

My Best Friend and Favorite Teacher

Mama taught seven grades in the mid-thirties in a one-room schoolhouse in South Carolina. On cold mornings she arrived early to build a fire in the pot-bellied stove so the children could enter a warm room. On hot days, she took her children outside under the shade of the massive oak trees where they would do their lessons and learn from their surroundings.

There was no running water in the building. Students carried in buckets of cool water from the well for drinking and for washing their hands. The privy was located at the back of the school.

There was no electricity in the building. On dark, overcast days, the students would move closer to the one large window that provided the only source of light.

Mama practiced site-based management. She used peer tutoring, cooperative learning strategies, an integrated curriculum, multi-aged grouping, seminars, hands-on activities, and environmental studies long before the current names were given to these approaches to teaching and learning.

I was her youngest student, for she was pregnant with me at the time. I have continued to learn from her ever since.

Acknowledgments

For most of my career, I held positions that gave me the opportunity to visit teachers' classrooms to observe and participate in the good things taking place there. This book is about those *good things* and the exceptional teachers whose actions in the classroom paint a vivid portrait of effective teaching.

The focus of this book is on practice rather than theory. My research took place, for the most part, in the classroom with schoolchildren and teachers as the primary resources. I will always be indebted to the principals and teachers who welcomed me into their schools and shared their students, classrooms, concerns, hopes, and dreams.

In addition, I want to thank the many educators who, through interviews, conversations, letters, and responses to requests and questionnaires, offered the benefit of their teaching experiences and expertise. Some of their names are mentioned in the resource section. Their gracious contributions made this book possible.

Introduction

There is a universality of teaching. One becomes aware of this when observing or talking with teachers at school faculty meetings, national or international educational conferences, or just over a cup of coffee. We talk the same language; we walk the same paths. The bottom line in our profession is and always will be our students and how we can help them be the best they can be.

Good teachers love to share stories of what is going on in their classrooms. They pick each other's brains, beg and borrow ideas from one another, and constantly have their antennae attuned to better ways of serving their students.

They know the *real* action is in the classrooms, and teachers would love to visit other classrooms to investigate different teaching methods or strategies. However, teaching is a fairly isolated profession. There is little time or opportunity for teachers to observe other teachers, programs, materials, and classrooms, even within their own buildings.

I have been extremely fortunate in my career to visit countless classrooms and see the exciting things that are happening in them. This is my opportunity to share them with you.

Part I

CALLING
THE ROLL

Meeting the
Students and Teachers

Beth Smithson, Artist

"All eyes up here, please!"

All twenty-four pairs of eyes moved
from what they were doing
to focus on their teacher.

"Good morning, boys and girls.
It's time to begin."

And they did.

All Eyes Up Here!

In today's ever-changing society, our young people are often confused, disoriented, and frightened. They are confronted with violence, drugs, dysfunctional homes, abuse, loss, and death. In this atmosphere, the school is often the only safe haven they know.

And who is primarily responsible for establishing this haven? Eyes turn toward the classroom teacher to provide a stable environment for the child to grow, learn, and gain the skills necessary to someday build a better world.

This is an enormous task for the teacher. It requires love, knowledge, insight, skill, empathy, talent, understanding, experience, humor, and in many instances, blind faith.

The teacher, however, is up to this task. In my twenty-five years in education, I have visited many schools and classrooms and had the opportunity to meet and observe superior teachers. During the last few years, I have noticed an increase in teacher involvement in site-based management, improved and ongoing staff development and training, and the innovative use of technology as a tool for both learning and management. Classroom teachers are in various stages of employing higher levels of thinking and reasoning skills with students, increasing their use of cooperative learning approaches, providing hands-on experiences in math and science, and developing an integrated and more meaningful and relevant curriculum.

This book is not intended to be a "how to" book for teachers because most teachers already know *how to*. Recipes for teaching won't work, for individuals who desire to be effective teachers must incorporate their own personalities and styles into the basic tenets of good teaching. Nevertheless, teachers, whether beginning or experienced in the profession, must be knowledgeable of and competent in those fundamental *basics* and need to review them from time to time. From this solid foundation, they can continually enhance and fine-tune their skills to become even better teachers.

This book will provide an insight into the complex art and science of teaching. On one hand, we will look at the necessary nuts and bolts of the profession. We will review the classroom management and instructional strategies that help build the organizational framework in which effective teaching and learning can take place. On the other hand, we will look into the heart and soul of the profession to see the personal and professional qualities that make certain teachers so significant and memorable. We will examine the special relationships that form between teachers and students and between students and learning.

All eyes up here, please. We are ready to begin.

Handle With Care

"If you don't like kids, get out of teaching!" A simple admonition, but so true since our entire profession is centered on children.

Kids come in all sizes, shapes, colors, and dispositions. We have big ones, little ones, tall ones, short ones, fat ones, and skinny ones. They arrive at our door in a rainbow of colors. Some wear happy faces; some do not.

And let's face it. Some kids are not so likable all the time. There are noisy ones, angry ones, hostile ones, dirty ones, sneaky ones, greedy ones, arrogant and impudent ones.

Yet when they enter the classroom, these children are **ours**. All must be treated with love and respect. Their problems become our challenges. We accept the boy with the worn, torn, dirty clothes in just the same way as the little girl in the brand new pink ruffled dress. We have no favorites among our children. All must be handled with care.

Teachers, too, come in all sizes, shapes, colors, and dispositions. We have big ones, little ones, tall ones, short ones, fluffy ones, and skinny ones. They arrive with a wide range of experience, awareness, education, and knowledge of child development.

Some teachers are bubbling over with enthusiasm for their students and subjects; others have burned out. Some teachers are energetic and positive; others are tired and grumpy. Some teachers show children love and respect; others might embarrass or humiliate them. Some teachers act as though they never were children; but thank heavens, most still remember and understand.

A child can often sense if a teacher does not appear to like him. A shrugged shoulder, raised eyebrow, or sigh of exasperation can alert a child to the true feelings of the adult.

It is disheartening to feel unliked or unacceptable, and many children carry these rejections with them for years. In interviewing children and adults about their former teachers, I found that memories are clear and emotionally charged even decades later about how teachers once treated them:

> *She accused me of stealing the money. Although I had nothing to do with it, she never believed me. She slapped the palm of my hand with a ruler when I tried to explain. It made my face burn.*

> *My third grade teacher didn't like me. She never smiled at me. I always raised my hand to answer, but she never called on me.*

> *My teacher screamed at me in front of the whole class. She said that I was just a big baby. It embarrassed me so much that I pretended to be sick the rest of the week so I would not have to go back to school. I still remember how terrible I felt that day.*

These are examples of some of the sad or unfortunate stories related to me. Nevertheless, for every one of these, there are hundreds of heartwarming stories where teachers went far beyond the call of duty to help children and build their self-esteem. These stories are often not publicized for they are *expected* from our unsung heroes.

Perhaps the role of the teacher is best summed up by the late Haim Ginott, the well-known child psychologist, educator, and author, in his book, *Teacher and Child.* I have shared his words with my fellow teachers over the years and with my student teachers at every university orientation session. They have become part of my philosophy of education, and I hope, part of theirs:

> *I have come to a frightening conclusion. I am the decisive element in the classroom. It is my personal approach that creates the climate. It is my daily mood that makes the weather. As a teacher, I possess tremendous power to make a child's life miserable or joyous. I can be a tool of torture or an instrument of inspiration. I can humiliate or humor, hurt or heal. In all situations it is my response that decides whether a crisis will be escalated or de-escalated, and a child humanized or de-humanized.*

Let us be the instruments of inspiration to our students.

What Are Teachers Made Of?

Teachers are made of laughter, gold stars, smiley faces, Happy Grams, and good notes written to Moms.

They are sprinkled with silver and gold glitter and splashed with an assortment of finger paints in a rainbow of colors.

Teachers are made strong to withstand the wear and tear of children's hand prints, sticky kisses, and hugs.

They come with an endless supply of sugar cookies, jellybeans, and bandages.

They wear bright colors and carry tote bags filled with books, ungraded papers, lunch, lesson plans, sneakers, and treats.

Teachers are given special skills for mending broken hearts, understanding hurts, seeing out of the back of their heads, and looking into children's souls.

Their hearts and minds are filled with the joy of reading, a thirst for knowledge, and a passion for teaching which they eagerly share with anyone willing to listen.

Teachers are given the special gift of touching lives which is generously used to inspire young people to be the best that they can be.

Use All The Colors in Your Crayon Box

The entire topic of the "art of teaching" is a fascinating one. One reason is because the concept is rather difficult to define. We know what the art of teaching is *not*. It is not just the nuts and bolts of our profession. It's not just the particular knowledge that we, as teachers, gain about our subject matter, the skills we teach, the management techniques that help us organize our days, or our discipline strategies. It's not any one of these separate and apart from the others.

The art of teaching is much more. It is that special way a teacher combines all of these skills with his or her instincts, intuition, beliefs, attitudes, values, sensitivity, and common sense. It is that unique ability of teachers to draw on all their resources to guide their students to success.

A passion for teaching . . .

I believe that the art of teaching has its roots in a teacher's passion for his or her profession and for both the subject matter and students. This passion overflows into everything he or she does, and teachers experiencing this can't wait to get to their classrooms in the morning. They're excited about their jobs. They love their kids. They are always thinking about new and better ways to instruct their students. They attend educational meetings and subscribe to professional journals. They truly enjoy what they are doing. Teaching is a major part of their lives.

The ability to teach in a creative way . . .

The art of teaching involves, at a minimum, three areas: the teacher's ability to instruct in a creative, informative, and interesting way; the teacher's ability to fine-tune his or her sense of timing that ultimately benefits the learner; and the teacher's ability to motivate and inspire students. There are obviously other areas in developing the art of teaching, but I believe these three are crucial.

Let's first examine the teacher's ability to instruct in a creative, informative, and interesting manner. Have you ever sat through a lecture that droned on for hours with no breaks and no opportunities to escape? I had to endure this once at an educational meeting where the speaker actually held his head down and read in a monotone from a prepared script. Some of the audience dozed off. Others doodled or made notes to themselves. Some of those sitting in the aisle seats slipped away.

Needless to say, nothing was learned in this meeting other than the fact that dull, dry, boring speakers do *not* hold your attention. But this, in itself, was a valuable lesson. Students in our classrooms are a captive audience. They are not given the choice of whether to endure us or slip away. Therefore, we owe it to them to make our lessons interesting and hold their attention.

Someone once said that the difference between ordinary and extraordinary is that little "extra." Teachers who are real artists in this profession do more than hold the students' attention. They captivate their charges with creative activities, interesting stories, and colorful visuals to enhance the lessons. They inject a little showmanship and some flair in their presentations. They understand the importance of humor. They involve their audience and play to it.

I am reminded of the story of two families who were invited one summer to two different Fourth of July picnics. Both were asked to bring a dessert. Each family decided to purchase a large white sheet cake from the local bakery. One family took the cake just as it was, and everyone at the picnic enjoyed it thoroughly. The other family decided to make the white cake unique for this particular occasion. They designed an American flag by decorating it with blueberries and cherries. Everyone at the picnic *Ooohed!* and *Ahhhed!* about the cake and decided to place it in the middle of the table as a centerpiece for the Fourth of July celebration (until time for dessert, that is!).

This simple story underscores the fact that both cakes contained the same staples (in education, the basics: language arts, math, social studies, science, art, music); but one cake had that little extra — that creativity, passion, showmanship, pizzazz (the art of teaching) that helped to make it more interesting for the audience for which it was intended.

Let's take another example that occurred in two adjoining classrooms in an elementary school. The students on this grade-level were discussing the major cities in the United States, their unique cultures, weather, modes of transportation, entertainment, and food products. In discussing San Francisco, the first teacher went "by the book" and included all the necessary facts and figures. Students read from their textbooks and discussed the main points from the teacher's outline for study of this city.

The second teacher brought in slides of San Francisco that belonged to her brother-in-law. She divided the class into groups and let them decide which topics they would like to research and later report their findings to the group. The students chose topics such as Fisherman's Wharf, Chinatown, the cable car system, the Golden Gate Bridge, Alcatraz Island, and the Napa Valley wine country. They wrote the Chamber of Commerce and the travel bureau to obtain information, pamphlets, and maps. The class invited three parents who had visited or lived in San Francisco to the class to give them firsthand information about the city. The students planned a culminating activity that included displaying posters of the city and preparing some real Chinese-American treats for their invited guests that included their parents, principal, and school office staff.

If you had the choice, which class would you sign up for?

The ability to develop a sense of timing . . .

The whole concept of timing is an interesting one that has fascinated stage and screen performers for years. We have all heard the saying, "timing is everything!" Teachers need to be more aware of its importance in the classroom. Some teachers instinctively know when to continue working on something and when to stop. They know when to change the pace of the lesson and when to shift gears altogether.

Let's look at some examples of how timing affects teaching. In the first case, I was observing a health class that was deeply involved in studying the skeletal system. Although interest was high, the students had been sitting rather long. The teacher glanced around, noticed that one or two students were getting wiggley, and asked the class to stand.

"We are going to do an activity about the skeletal system," she said. "We will work in pairs. As I call out the name of a bone, find this bone on your own body and place your hand on it. Check with your partner to see if your location is correct."

The students were able to move around and stretch, work with a partner, and have a little fun while still being involved in the lesson's objectives. Through the teacher's instincts in knowing when the students needed a change of pace and her expertise in creating a natural progression in the lesson to include the activity, she was able to keep the students interested and on task. **TIMING!**

The second example occurred in May when an ancient room air-conditioner was on the blink in a classroom I was visiting. It would gasp and sputter and choke and wheeze. It was obvious that it was terminal. The room was so stuffy and the noise from the air-conditioner was so distracting that it was difficult for the children to concentrate on the literature lesson that the teacher had just introduced.

"This afternoon we will try our hand at writing poetry," she began. "During the last few days, we've studied some really excellent examples of poetry, and now it's our turn to see what we can do."

The teacher divided the students into six sections. They were given their task of working together to write a poem about springtime.

"Now, we will get our supplies and quickly line up with our partners."

"Why are we lining up?" asked the students.

"Where are we going?" inquired another.

"We're going to the park at the back of the school," said the teacher. "What better place could we find to write about springtime? Now, hurry! Line up! Let's go!"

In the grassy area behind the school, the students formed their groups and sat under tall, expansive shade trees. Occasionally, you could see a group walk over to the flower beds or flowering trees to discuss a point or carry on research for their poems. Their new classroom was cool and a natural setting for their task. Creative juices were flowing. **TIMING!**

The last example is a story told to me long ago. Mary Jones was a second grade teacher in a small elementary school located on top of a mountain. Each year the school had their traditional clothesline art show and invited all the residents of the mountain to attend.

Proud parents and grandparents praised the children's masterpieces. All of the students worked hard on their creations, but year after year, Mrs. Jones' second graders' artwork seemed to stand out above all the others.

"Mary must have some baby Van Gogh's hidden in her room," said a fellow teacher. "Her students' paintings are always so clear, and the colors are so bold and vibrant."

"What's your secret, Mary?" inquired a grandparent who had also noticed how Mrs. Jones' class excelled each year.

"Oh, there's no secret," replied Mrs. Jones. "I just know *when* to take their paintings away from them!" **TIMING!**

The ability to inspire, encourage and motivate . . .

In addition to having a sense of timing and being able to teach in an interesting and enthusiastic manner, the teacher who displays a real art of teaching has the ability to inspire, encourage, and motivate students. When I think about teachers who truly inspire students, I think about a professor I was fortunate to have for a twelfth-grade English class at Mars Hill Junior College in North Carolina.

At the completion of my eleventh grade in high school, I needed only one credit in English to receive my diploma. Since I had already been accepted by Duke University and was anxious to begin my college life, I decided to enroll in an institution offering that course to complete the twelfth grade English requirement.

So I packed my bags and went to Mars Hill to get the one credit that I needed. What I received there during that summer of 1953 resulted in much more.

Professor Ramon DeShazo, or "Papa De" as we affectionately called him, was a very special person. He was a *no nonsense* kind of professor, but he had a sense of humor and displayed a real passion for teaching.

At Mars Hill, we attended classes in the morning and worked on research assignments in the library every afternoon and night. Papa De taught us about every nook and cranny in the library and made the reference books come alive.

He had high expectations for us, and he really made us work. But my memories are of Papa De working *with* us. His research assignments were difficult; therefore, we spent many hours in the library. When we began to have trouble with our work, we would look up and invariably see Papa De enter the library. Students would flock to him for suggestions and guidance. He always seemed to be in the right place, especially for us, at the right time. He would listen to each of our problems and give us a hint as to how to proceed. Later, he would get with us again to check our progress.

I think we took him for granted. Perhaps we believed, as most students do, that teachers not only work, but *live* in their schools. As a principal, I had many kindergarten and first grade students look around my office and ask me where my bed was.

Looking back now, I believe Papa De made a point of periodically visiting the library to check on his struggling charges and offer his assistance. He could have left us on our own. Some of us would have survived. But many of us would have become frustrated and perhaps, even given up. He was, however, a *teacher*, and he wanted to be there to guide, motivate, encourage, and inspire. To Papa De, the *process* was as important as the product.

Yes, I gained so much more than one lone high school credit during the summer that I was under Papa De's tutelage. I gained a deep respect for teachers based upon the qualities that Papa De exemplified. And I discovered my lifelong love for writing, reading, and research. I can't enter a library, even today, four decades later, without thinking of Papa De. And sometimes, when I'm working there and having difficulty with a writing or research problem, I still look up and expect to see him standing there, offering me encouragement.

My daughter is an art teacher in North Carolina. Once I visited a first grade class of hers. A little redheaded girl asked me to sit with her while she busily finished her drawing.

"Isn't it pretty?" she asked, admiring her artwork.

"It certainly is," I agreed.

"Do you know *why* it's so pretty?" she asked.

"Well, your drawing is bright and has lots of pretty colors," I commented.

"That's because I used all the colors in my crayon box," she said, grinning from ear to ear as she divulged her secret to success.

Perhaps we, as teachers, also need to know how to use all the colors in our crayon box to paint a beautiful picture of our teaching. In addition to mastering our subject matter and having an understanding of the developmental stages of young people, we need to be aware of the importance of timing, humor, and creativity in the classroom and know how to encourage, inspire, and motivate our students to do the best they can. Perhaps all of these together contribute to what we call the *art of teaching.*

We Believe in Children

I was dashing from one elementary school to another while working with student teachers when I saw this poem hanging in the entrance hall of a school. I looked below the poem to see who wrote it, but it stated "author unknown." I like to think that perhaps a teacher wrote these touching thoughts:

We believe in children,
Little ones, big ones, thin ones, and chubby ones.
There is faith in their eyes, love in their touch,
And hope in their attitude.
We thrill with them at life's joys,
Bow with them in worship,
And hold them close in tragedy.

We believe in children,
The fragile dream of yesterday,
Life's radiant reality today,
And vibrant substance of tomorrow.
We believe in children, for wherever we go,
We find yesterday's children
Who were nurtured in love, truth, and beauty
At work trying to make this world
A better place for everyone.

Author Unknown

Do No Harm

When physicians enter the practice of medicine, they take an oath that outlines the moral and ethical standards expected of them in their profession. In the Hippocratic oath, the physician swears to use his knowledge only to save life, to hold sacred any confidences learned in the profession, and above all, to do no harm:

> . . . I will prescribe regimen for the good of my patients according to my ability and my judgment and never do harm to anyone.

Perhaps we in the teaching profession need a similar code of ethics. Before we walk into the school, greet our first student, or write "Welcome to Our Class" on the chalkboard, we need to promise to use our knowledge only to make life better for our students. We must make a personal vow to divulge no confidences gained in our profession, and above all, to do no harm.

No teacher ever sets out deliberately to hurt a child. Yet the words that we choose to use or even the subtleties in our reactions to certain students have the power to injure children emotionally. And these hurtful situations, though often brief in duration, may be long-lasting and severe in a child's memories.

Have you ever been called "clumsy" or "stupid"? Has anyone ever embarrassed you by asking, "Don't you ever listen? How many times do I have to tell you that . . . " Have you ever been personally attacked for something that you did or failed to do?

Let's take a look at a typical school situation and see how it was handled:

> A kindergarten child drops his lunch tray in the cafeteria.

> The teacher yells, "Marcus, this makes the second time this week! Why don't you look where you are going? I swear, you are so clumsy! Just like your brother!"

The teacher, in her brief tirade, has attacked the child, his ability, and his family. She has left little room for the kindergartner to redeem himself. And she has failed to solve anything.

Nothing, other than damaging confidence and self-esteem, can be accomplished by attacking the individual. Therefore, we must **attack the problem,** *not the child.*

Now let's take a look at that situation again:

A kindergarten child drops his lunch
tray in the cafeteria. He appears to be
quite upset.

The teacher walks over to the child,
leans down and helps him pick up the
items from his tray that are on the
floor.

"You know, it's not easy to carry these
trays when there's so much on them,"
the teacher comments. "Perhaps if we
move everything to the middle of the
tray, it will be easier for you to handle.
Let's try it and see."

In this situation, the child feels that he has
someone to help him and who understands his plight.
He also has received a concrete suggestion that may
help him the next time he carries his tray. He leaves
with his self-esteem intact.

In this case the teacher attacked the problem,
not the child. She helped solve the problem, hurting
no one in the process.

Above all, ***do no harm.***

An Exceptional Teacher

I loved to visit Caroline Ellis' kindergarten class. It was always a flurry of productive activity with so many interesting lessons taking place. Once I peeked in her classroom the week before spring vacation. In the library area, children in rocking chairs were browsing through Easter books. Others were creating bunny masterpieces at the art easels. Some were describing Peter Cottontail in their writing journals. Still others in the home living center were coloring pretend Easter eggs. Caroline was busy, as usual, monitoring the children at each of the centers, encouraging them with a smile here and a hug there.

For years the university placed a student teacher with Caroline. Perhaps they were trying to clone her. Caroline was a teacher who used every minute and happening as a teaching opportunity. The university knew that the students placed under her supervision would receive a wealth of good instructional experiences.

I asked one of my student teachers, Sandra Hughes, to jot down some things that she learned from Caroline during her eight weeks with her. The following are some of her thoughts:

> I've learned so much from Mrs. Ellis that it is difficult to put on paper what is in my mind and heart. First of all, I learned that you can have a happy day without ever raising your voice to a child. Mrs. Ellis shows that she really cares about children by using a positive tone and calling each child by his or her name.
>
> I have learned that children can have fun while they learn. I now know how important it is to fill each valuable minute of the school day with numbers, letters, science, poetry, art, music, the wonders of nature, and much more.
>
> I feel that the knowledge I have gained from working with this teacher and observing her teaching methods could never be learned from a textbook or lecture. This kind of knowledge is a combination of wisdom and years of experience coupled with love, care, and respect for children.

Caroline retired at the end of that school year. What a loss for our school system and the children who will never get to be in her wonderful classroom. But there are many Carolines in the various school systems throughout our nation, and Jacks and Marys and Beths and Freds and Joes and Petes and Paulas and Charlottes. What a blessing their careers are to the countless children who have been or will be their students and who will always remember them as exceptional teachers.

Magic and Miracles

There are teachers who through their creativity, initiative, and imagination make magic and miracles happen for children. Aaron Washington was one of those teachers.

I met Aaron my first year as principal of Saint Elmo Elementary School in Chattanooga. I immediately discovered that besides being an excellent math teacher for our sixth graders, he was also an accomplished musician.

I wanted to give children opportunities to perform, for I believe it helps them build confidence as well as school memories. So between my beliefs and Aaron's talents, we made a good team. Aaron could, after a few rehearsals and a few choice words, turn seventy-five wild and disorganized sixth graders into the Hallelujah Chorus.

Aaron was a magician, as well as a musician; he pulled many budding altos and sopranos out of his hat. I loved to watch him work with the chorus. The children never took their eyes from him. They watched his hands for cues to tempo and volume. They watched his facial expressions to see how they were doing. When he smiled, they smiled, because they knew that they were performing well.

Aaron asked me if we could have a Christmas program. I was all for it. I wanted the parents to attend and see their children perform. I told him, however, that since it was my first year as a principal, we wouldn't have any extra money for costumes or scenery. This fact did not deter Aaron, and he went full-speed ahead with his planning.

For the next few weeks, I was busy with the instructional program and the ever-dwindling school budget. Occasionally, I could hear the chorus practicing their songs. Every now and then I would duck my head into the music room to catch a few bars of a familiar tune.

Aaron met me in the hall one day. "Can the chorus wear robes for the performance?" he asked.

"I didn't know we had any," I replied.

"I think I can scare up some," he said.

"That's fine with me. I'll check with you later." And off I went to outline a better route for fire drills.

One week prior to the holiday program, I met with each teacher before classes began to make sure the children knew their speaking parts and verses to poems. I decided to drop by Aaron's room to discuss the choral selections and finalize any last minute changes with him. To my surprise, the room was full of children and teachers.

"Dr. Carr, come and see our robes," invited Aaron. "We've been meeting every morning before school starts to fit our costumes. We're just about ready for the big day." Aaron was on his knees with pins in his mouth, turning up the hem of one of the student's choral robes. Mrs. Vaughn and Mrs. Tindell, his colleagues, were busily helping him.

I stood in the doorway and just stared. There before me was an overflowing classroom of sixth graders in their "robes."

"Oh, my heavens!" I thought as I did a double-take. "They're wearing garbage bags—brown, plastic garbage bags! *Garbage bags!*"

"Aren't they beautiful, Dr. Carr!" exclaimed one student.

"Is mine too long?" questioned another.

"Am I next, Mr. Washington?" asked a sixth grader, taking his place in line.

I pulled Mr. Washington aside and whispered, "Aaron, aren't those—uh . . . uh . . . "

"Don't worry, Tee. They'll look great once I put the red bows on the front. Remember, we're not through yet."

"But, uh . . . you know, Aaron, this is our first

program, and . . . uh . . . lots of people are coming, and we . . . " I stammered.

"Oh, it will be beautiful, Tee. You'll see!" he said, beaming with pride, as he continued to pin and shape his creations.

I walked back to my office with my head down and my cheeks flushed. "How would parents react to their children wearing garbage bags?" I wondered. "As a first year principal, would I be drummed out of the corps? Given my walking papers? Shot at sunrise?"

Then I got hold of myself and thought, "They really don't look so bad . . . if you didn't *know* they were garbage bags. And the kids love them." Perhaps, I decided, the situation needed *help* rather than criticism from me.

I went behind the stage and examined the lighting setup. This was an old, dilapidated system, but I found it was possible to slightly dim the house lights. I practiced until I knew what I was doing.

The day of the program arrived. Parents and friends filled the auditorium. I stationed myself backstage and lowered the lights as the chorus marched slowly down the aisle, singing the first selection. Parents and grandparents strained their necks to locate their loved ones.

As the children moved, the robes rustled like taffeta and the soft lighting made the plastic shimmer and glow. The children turned at the front of the auditorium to face the audience. Proud, happy faces peeked out over large red crepe-paper bows.

Under Mr. Washington's direction, the members of the chorus sang like they had never sung before. I emerged from backstage to view the children. The choral robes were beautiful—a portrait of red velvet and brown taffeta. *Magic*—Aaron Washington style— was happening.

Goose bumps broke out all over me. This always happens when I witness a miracle.

Part II

FEELING SPECIAL

Helping Individuals to Take a Bow

Making a Difference

Lancaster, South Carolina, is my hometown. I am a product of the Lancaster Public Schools, and I am proud of the quality education I received there. When I saw a copy of the *Lancaster News Special Edition* entitled "In Celebration of Education," I was particularly interested.

It seems that the Lancaster County Public School System held an essay contest for students to write about their favorite teachers. The winning essays were printed in the special edition of the paper.

The results of these students' essays were quite revealing. They showed that it's not just good teaching that makes teachers special to students, but it's *the way teachers treat children* that makes the difference. Ernest Mathis, Jr., who was at that time the superintendent of the Lancaster schools, said of the essays, "You'll see over and over again how much the little things mean to our students—the hug, the card to a sick parent, the enthusiasm in class, and the smile after a tough test."

In reading these essays, several common themes emerged as characteristics of *favorite teachers*. The most prevalent was the belief by the students that their teachers would be available if and when they needed them. The students felt that they could talk to teachers about any problem, either personal or school-related, and the teachers would listen and understand.

Another theme that emerged was that their favorite teacher motivated and encouraged them to do their very best. The students' essays related how teachers helped them set high expectations and goals for themselves and then worked with them to help them achieve these goals.

A reoccurring theme in the essays was that the students believed their favorite teachers made them feel special. This resulted in the students feeling good about themselves and about their achievements in school.

In the essays, the students wrote about specific instances that endeared the teachers to them. One student related this incident:

> . . . he spent his own time after school to help me type the class paper on the computer.

Another stated:

> . . . she goes *beyond* the textbook.

A student commented:

> . . . he encourages us to express our
> opinions.

And one student echoed the feelings of many:

> She has a good sense of humor.

Almost all students described the positive learning environment in their favorite teacher's classroom. The following are some excerpts from the essays:

> In his class, it is a crime to say the
> word *can't*. He likes to get the class
> involved in different projects. We got a
> chance to watch tadpoles turn into
> frogs.
>
> In her room, imagination flourishes.
> She brought faraway lands right into
> the classroom.

Other students mentioned the patience of their teachers. One student said:

> She doesn't just ask you a question and wait just a second and then call on someone else, but she lets you *think* a minute.

Another mentioned the teacher's part in introducing him to new avenues of creativeness:

> She started me writing stories in the second grade, and that's the reason I love writing now.

Several first graders mentioned personal reasons for selecting their favorite teachers. One student said:

> Sometimes I'm afraid to tell when something bothers me, but when I do, she makes me feel good. She makes me not afraid anymore.

Another commented:

> She sends me a card for every holiday.

Another student related this story:

> When my mother was in the hospital to have surgery, my teacher would ask about her every day. When she saw me looking sad, she would call me to her desk and give me a hug — just like my mother would have done.

And another recalled the following:

> . . . she helped me pull my loose tooth
> and it didn't even hurt!

From these essays, we see that the things children remember and that give meaning to their lives are often the kindnesses shown to them by their teachers. And the majority of teachers, because of the sheer number of students that they work with in their busy school schedules, may not even remember the specific words or deeds that the students hold so dear.

Perhaps the message is clear. We must become more attuned to our own words, actions, and body language, and the positive and negative signals we are sending forth. And as teachers, we should take an extra moment to perform that little act of kindness that could possibly affect a child's life. We do not always see the immediate results of our behavior, but all that we do and say and feel as we go through life means something and makes a difference to someone. Throughout this book I have included portraits of teachers who have made a difference in the lives of individuals.

Everyone Needs a Cubby

I don't remember when I first heard the word "cubby," but I do remember how I felt when I heard it.

Some words give me a special feeling. Cubby is one of those words.

There are many words, I'm sorry to say, that are cold words. These are words that do bad things to your mind, body, and especially your spirit.

Hate is a cold word.
Fear is a cold word.
Hurt, fight, kill, scream, and mean are cold.

Love is a warm word.
Safe is a warm word.
Fuzzy, soft, baby, kittens, and mittens are warm.

Cubby is a warm word.

A cubby is a place that holds all the things that mean something to you. It is a safe, warm place that belongs only to you.

In kindergarten, you have a cubby. It is where you keep your coat, mittens, and rainboots. It is where you place your lunch box, snack-time cookies, and favorite drawings. There is even room for your teddy bear and blanket.

As you grow bigger, so does your cubby.

It becomes your room, then your classroom, then your school. It can grow to be your town and country. And then your work. It should always be your home and family.

It is a warm, safe place that holds and protects all the precious things that give meaning to life.

Everyone needs a cubby.

The Silver Frame

I never realized the importance of a note of kindness until one day when I, as principal of the elementary school, visited the home of one of my teachers who had been sick all week. The teacher called the school to tell me she would return to work on Monday, but she needed her manuals and lesson plan book to prepare her next week's lessons.

On Friday afternoon, I went by her apartment to take the books. We chatted for awhile and when I turned to leave, something caught my eye. There on the coffee table in a silver frame was a note that I had written after visiting her classroom a few weeks before. It said:

> Enjoyed visiting your classroom today! You really had the children involved in the story. I especially enjoyed the role-playing and lively class discussion!
>
> Sincerely,
> Tee

I left her apartment and drove home, still thinking about the note in the silver frame. It seemed to grow in significance and symbolize the importance of words of encouragement, support, and praise in our lives.

Many teachers and principals, over the years, have told me how much they treasure the notes of appreciation sent to them. One principal confided to me, "I keep my notes in my 'rainy day' box. When I have a frustrating or stressful day, I go home, fix a cup of hot tea, and reread my *fan mail*. The letters from my students are most cherished. They perk me up and in no time at all, I'm ready to face the world again."

A teacher commented, "I call them my love notes. And yes, I have all of them. I would never dream of throwing any of them away. You see, they can't be replaced."

I have always thought of myself as a positive person, for I can find the good in people and events. I've always supported and commended the accomplishments of the teachers and students under my supervision. However, most of my praise, up until this time, was verbal.

This event marked the beginning of my *note-writing* stage of life. Suddenly, written comments took on a new meaning for me.

While verbal praise is fleeting, written praise is long-lasting; where verbal praise is elusive, written praise is tangible. Written praise can be touched, held close, read again whenever we need a warm feeling or a little extra confidence, and even shared.

Written praise can be carried in a wallet, tacked on a bulletin board, taped to the door of the refrigerator, placed in a scrapbook, or mailed to your mother.

It can be xeroxed, enlarged, E-mailed, or faxed. It can *even* be displayed in a silver frame.

Poor Baby

Over the course of my career, I have listened to the problems of children, parents, teachers, student teachers, and other administrators. The problems have ranged from bruised elbows to bruised egos, from cuts on fingers to cuts in personnel.

For a brief period in my life, I believed that when people brought a problem to you they wanted help in finding a workable solution that would lead to some type of action. This, I've found, is not necessarily so!

I now realize that most people only want a *poor baby*. They want you to listen to them, show sincere concern, and empathize with their situation. They want a chance to sound off and unload their problems on someone they trust. Then, feeling better, they usually go about their business, relieved of some of their stress.

Children, in particular, need adults who will listen to them. They must believe that someone cares about their problems and understands that life can be difficult at any age.

I was visiting a school last fall when a kindergarten child ran to me and exclaimed, "Dr. Carr, I scraped my knee real bad and it bled and bled. Look at it!"

"Oh, poor baby, I'm so sorry," I replied as I leaned down to closely examine the knee that was decorated with a patriotic red, white, and blue bandage. "It must have really hurt."

"I only cried a little," she said as she rubbed her knee.

"I'm glad you're feeling better now. Do you need another BAND-AID®?"

"No, this one is okay. Got to go now! Bye!" And she gave me a brief hug around the neck and skipped off to class.

Someone had listened to her story. She had received a little attention and sympathy. She felt better. Life went on. Case closed.

The other day I told my husband that I was really stressed out because things were piling up on me, and I couldn't find time to finish all the projects that I had going. On top of all this, my computer had a terminal disease. And I felt fat. He listened carefully, thought for a moment, and replied:

> "You really need to place things in order
> of priority. Then attack one project at a
> time. And don't take on anymore
> projects until you've completed the ones
> you have. As to the computer problem,
> we better call someone today to fix it.
> And for Heaven's sake, quit getting on
> the scales!"

I listened to his advice and said, "You're right. Thanks, honey, I really appreciate your help." As I turned to walk away, I thought, "You know, all I really wanted was a *poor baby*."

I Was The Favorite

Once there were three sisters who traveled to their home town for the funeral services of their beloved mother. The three women were highly successful in their personal and professional lives, and they attributed their accomplishments, in large part, to the love and support they received from their parents.

After the funeral, the three daughters remained in their home town to renew relationships and reminisce about the wonderful times they shared as they were growing up. That night they told story after story about their mother. Suddenly the eldest daughter said, "I just can't hold this in any longer. I hope you won't be angry or hurt, but Mother always told me I was her favorite."

The middle daughter retorted, "I'm sorry, but that *can't* be true. Mama said I was her favorite, but she made me promise I wouldn't tell. She thought you two might get jealous."

The youngest daughter let out a robust laugh and blurted out, "Well, you're *not* going to believe this, but Mama always told me that *I* was her favorite! Of course, she swore me to secrecy, too!"

Then the three "favorite" daughters hugged each other and laughed and laughed until tears came into their eyes. The youngest looked upward and said, "Oh, Mama, you rascal!" Then they continued to share stories about their mother and her *unique* ability to make everyone feel special.

From the beginning of our careers, we are told that we must have no "favorites" among our students. All children should be given the same respect, love, understanding, patience, and attention.

But no one ever told us that we could not have ALL favorites in our classroom. Just imagine a room full of children where each child knows - yes, *knows*, that he or she is your favorite student. Each child thinks that you treat him in a special way and that his potential is limitless. Yes, these children will go far and accomplish much, for they are s*pecial.* Now, multiply each child's confidence and capacity for growth times the number of children in your classroom who are all thinking, *"I am the favorite!"*

I Am Important!

All children need to feel special. My philosophy as a teacher and later as a principal was to focus on this belief and try to find ways for students to feel important and valued.

Sometimes it takes so little, but it means so much to a child. The following story will show how true this is.

Carrying the Box

The daughter of a friend of mine came home from school and announced that she had been given a wonderful part in the school play. "I get to carry the box," Kim exclaimed proudly.

Not really understanding the significance of this part but not wanting to dampen her daughter's spirit, the mother replied, "That's great, Kim! I know you're happy!"

Kim was so elated that she begged her mother for a new dress for this special occasion. Her mother got busy and spent several days making her a beautiful dress.

The night of the school play arrived and excitement filled the air. Kim's mother sat through endless acts, waiting expectantly for her daughter to appear. Finally in the last act, Kim walked on stage. She was in the middle of a large group of children bringing gifts to the Princess. They were all carrying large, beautifully wrapped boxes that they presented to the main character.

Then the children, with the exception of my friend's daughter, exited the stage. Kim turned to the audience, smiled brightly, waved to Mama, and curtsied twice before leaving the stage.

Kim's part had no lines in it and had lasted less than seven seconds, if you didn't count the several bows she took. But to Kim, it was her big moment in the spotlight. She would always have the memory of knowing she was special because she had been given the opportunity to "carry the box" in the school play. And Mama could not have been prouder if Kim had landed the lead role in a Broadway musical!

Wise teachers know that adding an extra part here or there in school plays will give more children opportunities to perform. Once we had a student who believed he "couldn't carry a tune" and didn't want to sing on stage with his class. Rather than place the boy in an embarrassing position, his teacher decided the class needed a flag carrier for their performance. Guess who was assigned that role!

All individuals, whether they are big people or little people, need to have their moments of glory. Sometimes those moments tend to *jump-start* us and give us the psychological energy to do even greater and more meaningful things in our lives. It is possible that the little girl who carried the box or the little boy who held the flag may go on to accomplish great things that could affect the world.

The Blue Ribbon

Ernest T. Washington was undoubtedly the worst kid in the fourth grade. In fact, he was probably the *worst* kid in the school. He was always getting into trouble — punching other students, talking back to teachers, yelling out in class, and consistently being in the wrong place at the wrong time. Ernest was also the shortest kid in the fourth grade. Some teachers thought he acted up because he was defensive about his small size.

Ernest's mother became a fixture in the school. She was constantly being called to school for parent conferences. Teachers pleaded with Ernest's Mama for help. Mama lectured to Ernest. She fussed at Ernest. She threatened him. She spanked him. But Ernest always said he didn't do it. No matter what the offense, Ernest didn't do it. He didn't know what all this was about. He was innocent. (Sure!)

One morning Ernest's mother hid outside the classroom door, hoping to catch her little darling in the act. Sure enough, Ernest was true to form. When the teacher's back was turned, Ernest turned a frog loose in the classroom. Girls screamed and jumped up on the desks. Boys laughed and hollered!

All at once, Ernest's mother tore into the classroom and jerked Ernest up by the back of his neck. She threw his trembling body into the hall. Steam protruded from Mama's nostrils. Her eyeballs turned white hot. Her hair crackled with electricity.

She yelled and screamed and called him everything but Ernest T. Washington. Then she rolled him into a ball and bounced him down the hall. Next all five feet-three of her jumped up and slam-dunked that little terror through the transom over the fourth grade door.

Teachers left their classrooms and congregated in the halls with their hands over their hearts. Roman candles exploded in the sky above the school. The National Anthem burst in the air. The frog jumped out the window. Flags were flying! It was truly a sight to behold!

Then Ernest's mother, exhausted and gasping for air, was helped down the steps and to her car. Teachers proudly hailed her as she drove away. But when her car had barely turned the corner, Ernest wasted no time in returning to his old ways of causing pandemonium in the classroom. Ernest's teacher threw up her hands in despair and began crossing off the days on her calendar until her retirement date.

A few weeks later, however, something magical happened. The Good Citizenship ribbons were presented in the school auditorium. Teachers noticed Ernest gazing at one of the shiny blue and gold ribbons. His eyes lit up. His feelings were obvious to everyone. He craved the ribbon. He coveted the ribbon. Somewhere in his mind, he decided that some day the blue and gold ribbon would be his.

And suddenly, Ernest changed his ways. He began to act like the other students. He began to say please and thank you and yes sir and pardon me and I'm sorry. He said good morning to the principal and opened the door for a teacher. He picked up trash even when it wasn't his. He stayed late in the afternoons to help straighten his classroom. He began to act like a real human being . . . some would even say, like a *good citizen*.

Teachers could not believe what they were seeing. "I know I'm dreaming, but don't wake me up," said the librarian, who had experienced more than her share of problems with Ernest T. His teacher had a change of heart and decided that she would probably teach a few more years. She called Ernest's mother to come to school, but this time for a *good* conference.

Yesterday, Ernest was awarded the Good Citizenship ribbon. When the principal called his name, Ernest came forward with a big smile on his face and had the shiny blue ribbon pinned on his shirt. Everyone applauded for Ernest, and one teacher was heard to whisper, "Now I've seen everything!"

Ernest T.'s mother was sitting in the front row grinning from ear to ear. "That's my boy!" she said, elbowing the parent who sat next to her.

What a day to remember! Perhaps it was just an illusion, but many people commented later that as Ernest left the stage, he walked a little taller.

You probably noticed that I exaggerated a little about Ernest T. and I definitely oversimplified the point of the story. We all know that there are Ernest T.'s in every school. There are as many causes for their inappropriate behavior as there are individual cases. And sometimes, even with our best intentions and efforts, we fail to reach them.

But often, as depicted in this story of "The Blue Ribbon," if these children are given something to strive for, to work toward, to aspire to that will make them feel more important, we can witness a positive change in their behavior. And it is up to teachers and principals to find that *something* that can affect a change.

In the following section on classroom management, we will discuss the ways successful teachers establish classrooms that are conducive to teaching and learning and that prevent, or at least diminish, problems that students like Ernest T. Washington help to create.

My Favorite Teacher

The Beginning and The End
by
Linda W. Knowles

I feel very fortunate to have had many excellent teachers, but the one I remember most is my first grade teacher. Every morning she stood at the door and welcomed us to her world of learning. She mainstreamed students because there were no special education classes. She taught us to work in cooperative groups because we needed to help others and to listen to others. Her loving, caring ways made each of us feel very special. I knew that I was "teacher's pet," and I think now that every child in that class probably thought the same thing.

In those days school always meant major productions, especially at holiday time. Our first grade play was the story of Christmas. Everyone in the class had a part and since I was a cute little curly-haired youngster, I was chosen to be one of the "host of angels." Our costumes were complete with wire gossamer wings and halos. Just as we finished our lines and the choir of little voices began "Hark, the Herald Angels Sing," the curtain was to close. Unfortunately, I was not standing exactly where I should have been and as the curtain closed, my wire wings caught and this angel took flight! I had so many crinoline petticoats on that I was not hurt but my teacher was so worried. She called and came by my house several times during Christmas vacation. I thought I was really something!

Eleven years later as I hurried down the hall to find my twelfth grade American history class, who should I find standing at the door but that same wonderful teacher. She had completed secondary certification and returned to teaching at the high school level. Once again, she was able to work her magic and history came alive for this group of seniors, many of whom she had started in first grade.

Part III

GETTING IT ALL TOGETHER

Effectively Managing the Classroom

If You Can't Catch 'Em

"If you can't catch 'em, you can't teach 'em" is a familiar saying among educators. Every time I hear this I think of the story my mama told me about a young student teacher who was interning in her school.

Mama said the student had confided that she really didn't want to be a teacher but was afraid of disappointing her parents. She believed they would be quite upset if she changed her mind about her career at this stage in her education. Mama said that on several occasions, Kristi had tears in her eyes even before the school day began.

One afternoon Kristi ran into Mama's classroom, screaming, "Mrs. Carnes, come quick! They're climbing out the windows!"

Mama told her students to continue working, and she quickly dashed across the hall to Kristi's room. Sure enough, the window was open and two boys had already "gone over the wall" to the playground outside. Two more were helping the rest make their great escape.

The student teacher was sobbing hysterically.

The first graders were giggling and pushing each other.

And my mother, who is normally a sweet, kind, loving, mild-mannered individual suddenly turned into a tough Parris Island Marine drill sergeant.

"GET BACK IN HERE IMMEDIATELY!" she ordered, "AND CLOSE THAT WINDOW. I mean *NOW!*"

Then she began to count: "ONE, TWO . . . "

And before Mama could say "THREE," the children had flown to their seats and were sitting in all innocence with their hands folded and their eyes up front. Mama directed Kristi to round up the two boys who were AWOL. Then Mama took another look at the little angels, nodded her approval, and all was right with the world.

That weekend, Kristi talked to her parents and subsequently changed her major. She told Mama her parents were very supportive and understanding and just wanted her to do what she wanted to do.

Our latest news about Kristi is that she is living in Charlotte, North Carolina, with her husband and two daughters and has a wonderful career in the *business* world. She apparently is quite happy in her new profession since she no longer has the responsibility of "catching 'em."

Classroom Management

Kristi's story underscores the importance of effectively managing the classroom. The entire realm of management is a complex, but crucial area in teaching. It involves everything that has an impact on the process of teaching and learning. It includes the way a teacher handles the physical setting of the classroom, the instructional environment, and the policies, procedures, and routines necessary for the successful day-to-day operation of the class. It is the teacher's way of "getting it all together" so effective teaching and learning will result.

Over the years teachers have developed strategies to make the students' time in the classroom more productive. These strategies have been based on sound educational research, tried and true classroom tips passed from teacher to teacher, and just plain old common sense practices.

Classroom management techniques should be periodically reevaluated and modified. What works for one group of students may not work for another. A student's age, maturity, and interests are all factors to consider when planning the best management practices.

Three Important Areas

On the following pages, we will look at three areas of classroom management: the classroom setting, the teacher's qualities and strengths, and the classroom rules, routines, and procedures. Think about *your* classroom, *your* students, and *your* style of teaching when deciding what will work best for you in establishing an environment for quality instruction.

The Classroom Setting

Classrooms should be inviting.

Let's look at the environment in which learning will take place. What should it communicate to the student? First of all, the classroom should be inviting and make students want to become a part of the activities taking place there. Interest areas such as an aquarium, pictures, posters, plants, computers, a science corner, or a library section will attract and hold their attention.

Think "personalization" when creating your room environment. Help children become a part of their new room by the creative use of bulletin boards, learning centers, and reading areas. An example of how to turn your bulletin board into a welcoming tool would be to take pictures of students on the first day. Most individuals, from kindergartners to teenagers, like to see their pictures displayed.

Students also like to see their names. Many teachers welcome the students by posting their names on the classroom doors. In the early grades, teachers place students' names on cards or sentence strips on their desks. In the upper grades, some teachers use name tags for the first few days to help everyone get acquainted.

In planning interest areas in your room, break away from the norm, if possible. Students are stimulated by their surroundings so try to have something that is unique. Make a creative area for independent reading by arranging pillows or bean bag chairs on the floor. One teacher made a cozy reading area by placing some lamps and rocking chairs on an area rug. Another brought in an antique tub filled with pillows for the corner of her room. Another teacher asked several of her parents to build a reading loft in her room to serve as a special place for her boys and girls to enjoy their books.

One word of caution: try not to go overboard when decorating your classroom because you don't want the room to appear cluttered or too busy. Too many items on the walls tend to distract students from their work. Periodically, check your room to see if any posters or charts need to be removed and either stored away or discarded.

Classrooms should convey messages.

In addition to being inviting, the classroom should convey a message. It should tell a story about what is taking place in that room. A glance around the room should tell you that this group is studying about "weather." The bulletin boards, learning centers, and student displays of class work should all be timely and relative to the topics being discussed.

Classrooms should also convey the message that they are student-centered. Young people spend a great deal of their time in school; therefore, the classroom should be theirs. Students should be involved in all aspects of classroom living, from designing bulletin boards to establishing their own rules.

Classrooms should inform.

And finally, the classroom should inform the students. Most teachers have large calendars, handwriting charts, and posters depicting various skills on the walls. They display classroom rules and daily schedules. In kindergarten and first grade classrooms, teachers label items (chair, table, door, aquarium) to help students increase their vocabulary. In all grades, storage containers should be labeled so students will know where to return items. Homework assignments and extra credit options including the dates the work is due should always be posted for the student's information.

Ten Questions About Your Classroom

Let's look at the physical arrangement of the classroom. As a teacher, how would you answer the following questions?

1. Are the desks arranged so you can easily walk between them to monitor your students' work?

2. Do you have clear visibility of each area in your room so you can observe what the students are doing at all times?

3. When you are teaching, can you see each student's face? Can each student see you?

4. Can students see the chalkboard without having to move their desks or strain their necks?

5. Are the traffic paths in the room wide and unobstructed? Can you line up easily for lunch, physical education classes, fire or tornado drills?

6. Are materials stored in a central location? Are they labeled for easy retrieval and return?

7. Is the pencil sharpener situated *away* from the students' seats and the main teaching areas?

8. Does each student have his own labeled "space" where he can hang his coat or store his books, lunch, or personal items?

9.   Do you have interest areas in the classroom for books, art or special projects, and learning centers?

10.   Can you change the seating arrangement with a minimum amount of noise if you want your students to work in pairs, cooperative groups, or teams for various activities?

If you can answer "yes" to most of these questions, then you are on the right track to good classroom management strategies.

Evaluating your classroom space . . .

Teachers usually do not have control over the amount of space their assigned classrooms contain. Too often, the rooms are poorly designed and limited in usable space. Electrical outlets may be located in the wrong places. Cabinets or lockers may decrease wall space. All of these obstacles can be frustrating when setting up classrooms. Nevertheless, try to keep in mind the following recommendations when you are evaluating the space that you have and attempting to enhance the physical setting of your classroom.

The physical arrangement of the classroom should . . .

- **provide a setting that is safe and orderly.** The teacher and students should be able to move without tripping over books, furniture, or each other. Exit areas should never be obstructed.

- **give easy accessibility to materials and supplies for both teacher and students.** Having to look for needed supplies is a waste of valuable instructional time. Storage containers should be clearly labeled, and students should be expected to return items to the designated areas.

- **guarantee clear visibility between the student and teacher and between the student and the teaching areas.** Better instruction and management practices result when students and teachers can easily see each other.

- **allow adequate space** for the teacher to monitor, the students to work, and for the desks to be moved, as needed, for more flexible seating patterns.

The Teacher

Although the physical setting is important, the key to good classroom management is the teacher. I have observed excellent lessons that took place under the worst conditions. My first classroom as a Title I Support Reading teacher was a supply closet with one small window. Other teachers I have known have taught their students on a stage, in a partitioned-off hallway, and at the back of an auditorium or cafeteria. Art teachers are often asked to teach the population of an entire school from a cart that is rolled from room to room. Music teachers usually have no space to call their own.

Through the years, teachers have had to endure inadequate classroom space, poor heating and lighting, insufficient materials, and out-of-date textbooks. Yet many of these same teachers have exceptional, well-organized classrooms where students make great strides in their educational progress.

Successful Management Strategies of Teachers

What characteristics of classroom management do successful teachers have in common? What are some things that they do in the classroom that ensure them a more productive day? The following are some practical suggestions that have resulted from observations and interviews with outstanding classroom teachers as well as from educational research.

Plan your lessons with care.

Have a clear idea of your instructional objective(s) and how you plan to reach them. Always over-plan in case the students work at a faster pace than you anticipated. Every minute spent in planning will pay off in dividends for you. Someone once said, proper planning prevents poor performance.

Have all materials for the lesson organized and easily accessible.

Nothing is more distracting than to have to stop the momentum of the lesson because of insufficient supplies or books. Have the necessary materials in front of you when you introduce the lesson.

Get the students' attention before you begin.

The most effective teachers have a "signal to begin." This signal can be something as simple as walking to the front of the class, pausing a moment and saying, "I am ready to begin" or "Please, may I have all eyes up here?" Many teachers say, "Please clear your desks and get ready for math."

I observed a sixth grade teacher who began each lesson by holding up his hand and saying, "Give me five!" This signal communicated to the students to respond by holding up their hands and giving the teacher their full attention.

After you establish the signal, instruct the students that when they hear this signal, they must stop what they are doing and give their full attention to you. Remember to pause for a few seconds after giving the signal so the students will have time to respond to it.

Effective teachers usually spend the first few days of the school year emphasizing this signal and preparing their students to listen for it. One teacher did this by letting her class play a game similar to "Freeze!" When the students heard the teacher's signal, they would immediately stop what they were doing (freeze) and turn their attention to the teacher.

Write your lesson topic on the board.

The topic of the lesson can be stated in a word or two (fractions, compound words, opposites). Writing it in large letters for all to see will help focus the students' attention on the subject. Many teachers take this a step further and use pictures, posters, or concrete objects to depict the topic.

A teacher who was introducing fractions, for example, brought in a real pizza delivery box with a cardboard pizza inside. He demonstrated how to divide the pizza into equal parts. Then he introduced an activity where the students ordered fractions of pizzas from their "pizza parlor." (Postscript: I'm sure I don't have to tell you that when this class successfully finished their unit on fractions, they celebrated with a *real* pizza party!)

Begin your lesson immediately.

This sounds like such a simple idea that it should be obvious and not necessary to mention here. However, let me share with you my script from an observation of a third-grade teacher who was experiencing classroom management problems:

> All right, now. Let's get settled down.
>
> Josh, where are you going? Sit down.
>
> Andrea, please turn around.
>
> Now, today we're going to . . .
>
> No, I said let's get our books out and get ready to . . .
>
> Today, we will talk about the effects of . . .
>
> Could I *please* have your attention? Thank you! Now today we will look into . . . *Who* is making that noise? Stop it!
>
> No, I don't want homework yet. Yes, I'm going to take it up but not right now.
>
> Thanks.
>
> Now, let's get back to our study of kinetic energy.

If you look closely at this script, you will find several problems that this teacher has. First of all, she did not seem to have an established signal to begin and never did get the students' attention. She had difficulty staying focused and was easily distracted by the students' unrelated questions. The students had no clue about the topic of the lesson until the teacher finally mentioned it at the end. Neither her lesson, nor her materials, seemed to be planned or organized. If you were her principal or supervisor, what steps would you take to assist her to become a better teacher?

Try to be consistent in your classroom routines and expectations for your students.

Students experience a sense of security and stability if they know what is expected of them. Teachers who constantly change the rules of the game are setting up themselves and their students for frustration, confusion, and possibly failure. This is not, in any way, to imply that there is no place for flexibility; however, major changes, if they are to be successful, should take place only after preparing the students by discussing the proposed changes and allowing the students to have some input in them.

Good eye contact and voice tone can go far in helping to manage students in your classroom.

An effective teacher can get a student back in line with a look or a whisper. Remember, there is no place for screaming in the classroom. It only makes the teacher appear to be out of control.

Stay focused on your topic.

Sometimes the best lessons can disintegrate if the teacher allows minor disturbances or unrelated questions or comments to interfere. I was observing a good lesson unfold on writing a friendly letter when the teacher glanced around and spotted a boy slouched in his desk, playing with his pencil.

"Mike, stop tapping that pencil, and sit up straight!" she admonished. "You're going to ruin your spine by sitting that way," she continued. Needless to say, all the eyes in the class turned to Mike to observe his deteriorating spine. And attention to the lesson was lost.

Keep your "teacher talk" brief.

Some lessons start off great. The teacher introduces the topic and gives directions for an activity that will take place. The students are motivated and attentive. Then something happens. The teacher continues to explain, and explain, and explain . . . Directions are repeated and repeated again. The kids lose interest. Some yawn in boredom. And attention is lost.

Once students are working independently, leave them alone and let them concentrate.

Sometimes teachers give students work to do independently, and then, a few seconds later, interrupt them with further directions or comments.

"You may begin working now," instructed the teacher and the children began their assignment.

The classroom was quiet, and the teacher moved among the students, monitoring their work.

"Could I have your attention just one more minute?" the teacher asked, interrupting the students. "I forgot to tell you that I want you to circle all the adjectives that you find."

Give the directions for the assignment, both orally and in writing. State the written directions briefly on the board or a chart so there will be no question about what the students are to do. Then let them work uninterrupted.

More often than not, teachers are the cause of their own management problems. Poor planning, not beginning the lesson immediately, stopping to look for necessary materials, or screaming at a student are surefire ways of losing control of the class. The teacher's talking too much, interrupting the students, and becoming distracted by minor disturbances are ways to lose the students' attention and interest. Once classroom control, attention, and interest are lost, they are difficult to regain.

Preparation and organization are the keys to good classroom management. Can you imagine twenty-five children trying to wait patiently and attentively while their teacher mumbles about not having enough glue or scissors ready for the art project and fumbles through her papers looking for the directions for it? Mumbling and fumbling are not conducive to a good lesson. Preparation and organization are!

In the next chapter, we will continue to look at effective classroom management practices. We will see the importance of rules, regulations, and routines to give the classroom structure and help it run smoother.

My Favorite Teacher

Is Kindness Out Of Style?
by
Julius Parker

For such a fragile thing, kindness is one of the strongest emotions known to mankind. It can literally make your day. It can put a warm glow in an otherwise chilly day.

Kindness doesn't need a by-product in order to be tangible. An act of kindness explains itself. So does a word of encouragement or a smile.

I vividly remember Miss Price, my first grade teacher at Park Place School. There was no preschool in those days, no transition to get a kid acquainted with the world of formal education.

I can still feel and see the reassuring smile that radiated from this wonderful lady. It said to me:

"You are in capable and caring hands. I am not your mother, but while you are in my care I will treat you as if you were my child because I love you."

I remember looking at that beautiful face and thinking how lucky I was to be in her classroom. "This must be what love feels like."

And the transference of love and care didn't stop in the first grade. There were other teachers who also knew how to pave the way for maximum learning. They realized their young charges needed a sense of self and confidence and would function better in a nurturing climate.

Miss Flynn, who taught Bible at Dickinson Junior High, was such a teacher. She realized her students were not only trying to learn but attempting to learn who they were and how they fit into the general scheme of things. Every day they made new discoveries, and beneath that challenging and contentious behavior, there were many questions about self and subject matter.

But when you walked into Miss Flynn's classroom, you felt a sense of peace and security embrace you. It was a safe haven created by this blessed lady.

I don't recall how she interpreted the Bible, but I do recall how her own peacefulness and calmness helped us through an exciting yet befuddling period of life.

Part IV

ESTABLISHING RULES, REGULATIONS, AND ROUTINES

Living Together in Harmony

Rules

Social studies classes in elementary schools teach us that if people in a community are to live together in harmony, they must adhere to certain rules, regulations, and routines. This same concept applies to a classroom which, in reality, is a small community.

The whole purpose of education is to help children grow to be decent and productive human beings. Therefore, we must have standards for behavior, and individuals must adhere to these standards. In our classrooms we have rules that students are expected to follow. Many of these rules are just guides for common courtesy.

Involve Students

The first few weeks of school should be spent in establishing classroom rules and procedures. It is imperative for the students to become actively involved in making their rules so they will develop a sense of ownership for them.

Some teachers set the stage for establishing rules by presenting classroom problems to students. They ask them to get into groups and discuss the problem and its possible solutions. The students then decide if a rule would be helpful in this situation. In some instances, they role-play the situation for the class both with the rule and without it.

A fourth grade teacher presented the following problem to her class:

> The teacher called on Mary Jo to give her book report. Four students in the back of the room were talking so loudly that Mary Jo was unable to complete her report. Most of the students in the class were angry that a few were being rude and embarrassing a fellow classmate.

The teacher then asked the students to discuss the problem and role-play the situation for the rest of the class. Some questions that the students addressed were, as follows:

- Should one group of students be allowed to disrupt a class activity?
- Should some people suffer because of others' rudeness?
- Could Mary Jo's grade be affected by the rudeness of these classmates?
- What rule would address this problem?
- How could it be enforced?

By addressing the problem in this way, students become involved in the processes of problem-solving and decision-making about their own community (classroom) life. By being part of the solutions, students are less likely to be part of the problems.

Keep Rules Simple

It is best to keep the rules simple and applicable to most situations. One school that I visited has only three rules, but these rules apply to just about everything that goes on in the daily lives of the students:

> Respect Yourself
> Respect Others
> Respect Others' Property

Think Preventive

Think "preventive" when deciding on rules. Proper management means reducing the number of potential behavior problems you may have to face. One of the best ways for the classroom teacher to think preventive is to mentally walk through the school day and pay particular attention to the times and places where problems could occur. Analyze these situations and try to think of better ways of organizing this part of your schedule, thus avoiding possible conflicts.

As an example, let's look at one of those times and how a teacher prevented a possible problem. Kids love to talk or whisper to each other when using the pencil sharpener. This can escalate into a push or a shove and eventually into a full-fledged discipline problem when students congregate in this area. Rather than have to deal with "who started it and who did what to whom," one teacher presented the problem to the class. The students discussed it and decided it would be easier for all involved to move the pencil sharpener to a location away from the other desks and the general flow of traffic. Along with this relocation, the teacher and students established a policy that only two people could be at the sharpener at any one time.

Limit the Rules

Teachers usually guide the students to limit the class rules to a number they can handle and remember. Let's look at the classroom rules of three different grade-level classrooms. Notice some of the similarities of these rules.

During a visit to a first grade room, I saw these rules posted in a prominent area:

> Follow directions.
> Show respect for others.
> Keep hands and feet to yourself.
> Talk quietly.
> Walk.

A third grade classroom had these rules displayed:

> Listen to others when they are speaking.
> Be prepared for your daily work.
> Stay in your assigned area.
> Respect others and their belongings.

Students in a fifth grade classroom worked together to develop a "classroom constitution." They signed a statement agreeing to abide by the four rules that *they* thought were necessary for a successful classroom.

Classroom Constitution

1. We will follow directions the *first* time given.
2. We will respect *all* people at *all* times.
3. We will be prepared for class and ready to learn with pencil, paper, books, and assignments.
4. We will remain quiet when someone enters the room.

Similarities

As you noticed from the above rules, they have some similarities. They were always stated in a *positive manner*. Instead of saying "Don't hit or kick others," it is better to state "Keep your hands and feet to yourself." Instead of saying "Never talk when others are talking," state "Be courteous when others are talking."

The rules were *limited in number*. Teachers believe it is best to have only four or five rules that can be easily remembered by the students. I visited one school that had rules for the classroom, rules for the cafeteria, rules for the playground, rules for the auditorium, and so forth. They added up to three pages of rules, sixty-nine in all. The students were overwhelmed by the number of rules they had to remember and obey. Obviously, this was not a workable approach.

The rules in the above examples were rather *broad in scope.* "Talk quietly" could apply to the cafeteria, the auditorium, or the classroom. "Stay in your assigned area" could apply to any area in the school to which the student is assigned.

In conclusion, rules that are limited in number, stated in positive terms, and broad in scope are more likely to be remembered and obeyed. You want to keep your rules as simple as possible and set yourself up for success!

A Tug of War

I once visited a sixth grade teacher who had a unique way to get his students thinking about rules. During an energetic session with his youngsters discussing the need for rules, he held up a jump rope and said, "Pretend this rope represents our rules. Now we can either have a tug of war over them or we can skip along together!" He demonstrated both actions, and the students tried to stifle their laughter at his attempt to jump rope. "So, let's get together in groups," he continued, "and come up with some rules that we can agree on and live with."

A lively discussion followed and the students arrived at five rules that they thought were necessary for them to live in harmony for the school year. Two students made a poster of the rules which they placed on the bulletin board.

"This system really works!" confided the teacher to me. "These rules are *theirs*, so they are more likely to abide by them. I hang the jump rope next to the poster. If someone breaks a rule, we point to the rope and say, 'Are we going to have a tug of war?' Usually, this breaks the tension," he continued, "and a grin and an apology follow! The kids believe that life is better for everyone around here when we *skip along together!*"

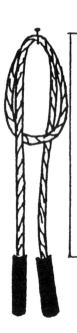

Classroom Rules

Be Polite
Respect others' property
Keep hands to yourself
Listen Carefully
Raise hands to speak

Consequences

Individuals must take responsibility for their actions; therefore, rules must have consequences if they are broken. Consequences for infractions of rules are often determined by the discipline committee in a school and are affected by the policies of the school.

Many school systems adopt a particular method of discipline or classroom management, and teachers are expected to follow this approach. We must remember, however, that what works well in one school area or with one particular grade level may not work in another.

Consequences can range anywhere from a verbal warning or time out to a loss of privileges or a phone call to the parent. I believe that consequences should be related to the specific infraction of the rule if they are to be meaningful. If a student, for example, writes on the restroom wall, he should have to erase and clean the damaged area. If a girl can't play with other children at recess without starting fights, she should lose her recess time to list the ways that she can change her behavior in order to get along with her peers.

Consequences, used in this context, help correct the problem by giving students a constructive way to make things right again. It also provides learning experiences for the students who must accept responsibility for their behavior.

Naturally, teachers must use their common sense with all situations. You don't want to roll out a cannon to kill a gnat. A simple "I'm sorry. It won't happen again!" will suffice for many minor infractions.

Students are becoming more and more involved in discussing and determining proper consequences for offenses. Some classes hold weekly sessions specifically designed to discuss problems related to behavior, rules, rewards, and consequences. Some schools, especially middle-schools, are implementing peer court systems in which students serve as jurors, attorneys, and judges to decide the fate of their peers. No matter what discipline program is instituted in your school, it is always best if young people perceive the program as fair and consistent and see its overall goals as preventive and corrective, rather than punitive in nature.

Rewards

We would like to believe that individuals will do the right thing just because it is the right thing to do. This is not always the case. Young children must be taught appropriate behavior.

Most teachers use some type of reward system to help shape student behavior. The following are some examples of rewards used by teachers:

Verbal praise for specific achievements
Good conduct certificates
Treats (stickers, candy, movie, popcorn or
    pizza parties)
Free time
Positive notes or phone calls to parents
Student-of-the-Week Award
A picnic or other outing with the principal

It's a good idea to check with students at the beginning of the year to find out what they consider to be a reward. Some classes would rather have a pizza party or a picnic on the playground than a certificate or blue ribbon.

The Teacher and Discipline

In any group situation, there can be misunderstandings, conflicts, and disruptions. This is true in a classroom. Tempers can flair, feelings can get hurt, and arguments often erupt. Students and teachers are human beings and they can get angry, upset, and frazzled at times. They must learn how to deal with their feelings so anger is not directed at other individuals.

Even in the best classrooms, rules sometimes get broken, and the teacher must intercede. He or she must have the skills necessary to deal successfully with discipline problems.

First of all, the teacher must *model good behavior.* Effective teachers should display a positive attitude, courteous behavior, and self-control. They must never allow themselves to be drawn into an argument with students. They must show that they value a classroom environment that is safe, orderly, and conducive to teaching and learning.

Next, teachers invite their students to *think preventive, rather than punitive.* They examine possible problems that could occur in the classroom with their students and try to think of ways to avoid conflicts. As we mentioned earlier, students may role-play more appropriate ways of behaving.

Effective teachers know that they must *attack the problem, not the child.* They never succumb to personal threats, blame, insults, sarcasm, or criticism. They do not humiliate or demean children. I do not believe that we have to beat kids down in order to build them up.

The whole point in correcting or shaping behavior is to move the students toward more self-control and self-discipline so there's no need to alienate or anger students in the process. I believe we can quietly inform students that their actions are inappropriate, counsel with them in private later, and together, agree on a more suitable manner of behaving in the future. Teachers must look at the problem rationally with the student and try to think of alternative solutions. Sometimes the fact that an adult is taking the time to work with a child individually to find more positive ways to behave may be the motivating factor that turns that child's behavior around.

In dealing with misbehavior, teachers find that it is best to *be brief, but firm.* It is not necessary to give a lecture or to give three reasons why this is inappropriate behavior. Just tell the student what you want him to s*top* doing and what you want him to *begin* to do:

> "Jerry, stop talking; get back to your book."

> "Meredith, turn around; finish your assignment."

Teachers *deal with more severe problems in private.* For example, if two students have a loud argument in class, the teacher stops the misbehavior, separates the two students, and tells them she will meet with them after class to discuss the problem. She does not interrupt the class further by chastising the students in front of the group.

Many teachers ask the offenders to go to the back of the room and write the reasons why this outburst occurred and how it could have been prevented. These written reports will be discussed in their meeting later. Then the teacher returns to her lesson.

Teachers *do not dwell on minor misbehavior.* Calling attention to minor misbehavior usually causes a greater disruption than the minor misbehavior does. Sometimes, just moving closer to the student while you continue to teach the lesson or placing your hand on the offender's shoulder will stop the problem. Sometimes, a "teacher look" will stop the misbehavior.

And finally, teachers *listen to students.* Many problems could be detected early before they escalate to major problems if only teachers would listen. Because it is impossible for teachers to listen to all students all the time, many teachers are placing a "Suggestion Box" or "Complaint Box" in their classrooms. This provides the students with a vehicle for communicating in writing with the teacher.

Remember, there are no "quick fixes" for discipline problems. To establish policies and procedures that are long lasting and productive, it requires a great deal of time, effort, patience, and sensitivity on the part of the teacher.

Regulations

Schools have certain regulations to which they must adhere. Regulations are usually principles, rules, or laws that are established to enforce the requirements of the State Board of Education and the local board of education. Copies of these requirements and policies are located in the principal's office and in the school library or teachers' lounge.

It would be to your advantage to secure these documents and study them. When reviewing local and state rules, you will discover that many regulations pertain to the organization and management of the classroom.

Routines

All institutions must have established routines if they are to operate in an orderly and productive fashion. People depend on these regularly scheduled activities and use them when they plan their own personal schedules. Think about the routines that are established in your community. In some cities, for example, trash is picked up on Monday and Thursday; the bank is closed on Saturday and Sunday; stores in the mall do not open until 10:00 A.M. Adults feel more secure in their daily lives when they know that certain activities will take place on a regular basis. The same is true for students.

If It's Thursday,
It Must Be Hamburger!

Schools need routines on which students, parents, and teachers can depend. Schools have a beginning and ending time, a calendar that denotes special holidays and vacation dates, semester divisions, and grading periods. Some schools are so organized that they send home weekly menus announcing the cafeteria lunches. In our school system, we used to laugh because we knew, "If it's Thursday, it must be hamburger day!"

Classrooms, also, need to have established routines. In addition to procedures to ensure safety such as fire and tornado drills, there should be routines to help the classroom operate in a systematic manner. Effective teachers know that time spent on planning the best methods for distributing supplies, heading papers, turning in completed assignments, and the many other necessary classroom functions, is time well spent.

When establishing any routine, make sure you have a clear rationale and keep the method simple. The whole point of developing these procedures is to simplify activities and save instructional time.

There are countless classroom procedures, some more important than others. You will need to decide on the routines that will enhance your situation and develop the best way for implementing them. On the following pages we will look at two that I believe are important, the routine for early morning instruction and the one for selecting classroom helpers.

Morning Routines

Let's look at a procedure that is working well in many classrooms. I've always called it the "Morning Routine." Some teachers call it a "Warm Up Exercise." Others call it a "Blast Off!" Generally, it consists of five to ten minutes of independent work that students complete during the first few minutes of class time each morning. The teacher places this work on the board *before* the students enter the classroom.

Rationale for this activity:

1. Provides an attention-getter or "think" problem for students to complete as soon as they enter the classroom.
2. Provides students an opportunity to follow written directions and work independently or with a group.
3. Provides a few minutes for the teacher to get the necessary housekeeping or secretarial duties completed.

Procedure:

1. The short assignment, related to current skills covered in the classroom, is always written on the board or charts prior to the students' entering the classroom.
2. Students read the directions and begin to work.
3. The assignment can be for individuals or small groups.

4. The completed assignment is always reviewed for accuracy by the student and teacher.

Let's look at an activity that was on the board in a fourth grade I visited. Think of the skills involved in this short assignment:

> You have just been chosen "Student of the Week" by the faculty at our school. You will be honored tomorrow at a special assembly program in the auditorium and presented a certificate and a free dinner for two at your favorite restaurant. You will be expected to make a short speech to accept this award.

Directions:

1. Compose your speech and remember to thank the members of the faculty.
2. Who would you take to dinner with you? Why?

Other teachers may present two questions each in a language, math, health, and science activity. The language part of this could include a skill on capitalization or punctuation:

Directions:

1. There are *seven errors* in the following sentences. Can you find and circle them?

A. i am going to visit joseph in san francisco
   california
B. my doctors name is dr harry jones

2. Compose a sentence that contains seven
   errors. Give it to the student who sits behind
   you for that person to correct.

One third grade teacher let her students solve
"Who-Done-Its?" based on plots and characters of
popular fairy tales and folk stories. Other teachers let
their students complete word puzzles, write friendly
letters to famous people, or compose invitations to class
parties or special events. Most teachers believed that
using a variety of activities was more motivational for
the students. The ideas for these activities are
unlimited.

One teacher shared her version of early morning
activities with me:

> I begin each day with the students
> working in groups to correct
> grammatical errors in quotes, poems,
> and stories that have been strategically
> placed around the classroom on
> sentence strips or construction paper.
>
> When the kids enter the room, they
> immediately get with their groups and
> begin to work on the problems. My
> students love to work in small groups,
> and since there is some movement
> involved in this activity, they don't
> consider it work.

Later, we come together in a large group
to compare results. It's important that
we get together to evaluate results and
bring some closure to the activity.

To summarize, these activities should center
around skills already introduced at some prior time
and should be a review. It is imperative that you check
this work with your students when they complete it. If
you forget to review it, the students will sense that it
was not important and they will lose interest in this in
the future. Allow students opportunities to work
individually, in pairs, or in small groups. And present
activities that are varied, interesting, challenging, and
creative!

Classroom Helpers

In my visits to classrooms, I notice that most
teachers designate at least two or three "helpers" who
assist during the day with various jobs such as taking
reports to the office, distributing papers and supplies,
and leading the other students to the cafeteria and
playground. This procedure works well, especially in
the lower grades.

As children get older, however, and can perform
more class duties, they should be allowed to assume

additional responsibilities. In studies of dropouts, many young people reported that they didn't believe they had a role in school. Too often, we believe that the students' role in school is just to *be there.* Not true! Students need duties that make them feel needed and respected as individuals.

I believe that teachers should *involve as many students as possible* toward the smooth operation of the classroom. The students, through teacher-directed decision-making and problem-solving processes, should decide what jobs are necessary. In addition, I believe the jobs should be performed on a *weekly,* not daily, basis.

Let's look at the rationale behind these suggestions:

1. Individuals want to be considered as valued members of a group. Their job title defines and enhances their value and gives them a sense of *specialness*: "I am the supply clerk" or "I am the line leader."

2. Most individuals are attracted to situations where they perceive they are needed. If students believe they have to be in class to perform a particular task and that other class members depend on them, they will make that extra effort to be there. Think how this could affect attendance rates positively.

3. A sense of ownership in the classroom will develop among students if they have an active role in its operation. This perception often leads to greater student pride in his or her surroundings.

4. By dividing the class jobs and spreading the responsibilities among all the students, a minimum of class time for individual students will be spent in performing these tasks.

5. By extending the span of time for job assignments from one day to one week, the student has an opportunity to develop a degree of expertise in performing the job.

All jobs should not be established at once. It is best to begin with the necessary ones and add others as the need arises. The teacher and students should take time to discuss and decide on the job descriptions. If necessary, the students could initially role-play the functions of the jobs as a way to establish and understand the responsibilities involved.

Martha Dyer Kaiser, a fellow educator and recipient of the Southeast Area (Tennessee) Teacher of the Year Award has this to say about involving students in the operation of the classroom:

> *I give the children in my classroom a lot of responsibility for the daily routines of the class and even for some of my work. You'd be surprised at what these students can*

do! When they are responsible for the workings of the class, they really feel a part of it.

It is beneficial to involve students in determining the classroom jobs, as they often see things in ways that we don't. This was exemplified by a first grade student who said he wanted to be the "back line leader." When questioned by his teacher as to what duties this person would perform, he quickly replied that this is the person "who keeps the back of the line straight and who closes the door after the other kids leave for recess and lunch."

Teachers who are trying this method of involving all students usually post a chart of the jobs with necessary space for writing in the weekly student assignments. They prefer to laminate this chart so they can use it over and over.

Two students could be assigned the job of entering the new names on the chart each week and making sure that each student is aware of his/her particular assignment. Two or three students could be designated as substitutes who fill in for boys or girls who are absent.

To ensure a smooth transition from one week to the next, let the experienced helper accompany or assist the new helper on the first day. This provides an opportunity for one student to have the experience of teaching his job to the novice. It also saves the teacher the time needed to train the new helper. Set a goal for all of your students to have active roles in the operation of the classroom.

In summary, the teacher spends much time and effort "getting it all together" in the classroom. Tasks such as establishing a positive learning environment, mastering the skills that help in managing the classroom, and setting up schedules, rules, procedures, and routines that help the classroom run smoother are mind-boggling, especially when you add these to the teacher's primary responsibility of teaching twenty-five or thirty energetic youngsters all day every day. Nevertheless, if we involve our youngsters in these tasks and make them feel more valued and necessary to school life, most management problems will decrease as the classroom truly becomes *theirs.*

My Favorite Teacher

The Teacher Who Changed My Life
by
Dalton Roberts

I was expelled from school in the tenth grade. And no injustice was done. I should have been expelled a year earlier.

After eight years of good grades, boredom, and purely external adjustment, I just broke bad. I hated school. I hated the seats, sitting down all day, the blackboards, the bells that never stopped ringing, homework, school work, and the teachers.

Yes, Mr. Burgner was justified in expelling me. I rolled waste baskets down the hall, stuck bobby pins in the edges of seats and twanged them with my foot, got into fights, smoked cigarettes in the boys room, put chewing gum on the seats in the girls room, hid snuff boxes full of sulphur behind radiators, skipped classes, played hooky, and turned a cow loose in the hall! Now, who would have thought a kid like that was worth messing with? Who would even try to help him? Lawrence L. Fults, that's who.

Mr. Fults was an awesome-looking man. At least, that's how he looked to me at the time, and other students seemed to feel the same way about him. Some of the boys called him "Adolph" because he had a shock of hair that fell down over his forehead. He tolerated no foolishness and would let the blade down on you quicker than a John Deere tractor.

He taught algebra, civics, and economics. Billions of people have lived upon this earth but not a single one has ever hated algebra as much as I did. I took algebra under another teacher and failed a semester. When I had to take it over to get enough credits to graduate, they assigned me to Mr. Fults! I shuddered. By this time, I had decided half-heartedly to try to graduate, but getting stuck in Mr. Fults' class took a heap of steam out of my compressor.

I stared out the window most of the semester and seldom did homework or the work assigned for class periods. He chewed me out several times but always told me I could do anything I set my head to do.

One day he told me to come see him after the final period. All day long I dreaded that final bell. I came within an inch of leaving school. But I went. He asked what was bothering me. I muttered some inanity. He offered to stay after school any day to help me. I thanked him but told him I just couldn't learn algebra. It was near the end of the semester and I knew I couldn't catch up. I had given up. On algebra. On graduation.

Report card day rolled around. Before the first bell rang, Mr. Fults came out where I was standing with a group of students and called me aside. "You know you haven't earned a passing grade in algebra," he said, as I looked down at the ground. "Yes, I know," I acknowledged. "What do you think I should do?" he asked, adding that he would like for me to look at him when we were talking.

I looked at him. To my surprise he didn't look angry. Just disappointed. I felt like such a rotten rat that I just couldn't answer him. He finally said, "You deserve to fail but I'm giving you a D-minus and I thought you might want to know why." "Yes sir, Mr. Fults, I would like to know why," I said, trying to contain my glee.

"Well, someday, you'll amount to something. You come from a good family. You've got a pretty good mind. You may even go to college. But you need that D-minus just to graduate so you can get into college. None of us deserve all the breaks we get in life and you don't deserve this one. You'll remember this one somewhere down the line."

You may not remember, Mr. Fults, but down the line I made an "A" in your economics course. Down the line, Sir, I remembered that break and made a "C" in college algebra, still hating it. Down the line I made an "A" in advanced statistics, detesting it but knowing I had to justify your confidence.

You were right, I remembered. And as I go on down the line I will keep remembering the teacher who turned my attitude around.

Part V

STAYING ON YOUR TOES

Strategies of Effective Managers

Staying in Touch

My husband, Jack Carr, was principal of Kirkman Technical High School in Chattanooga from 1961 to 1966. He was highly visible to his 53 staff members and 1200 students. Throughout the day, one could see him in the halls and classrooms and later in the cafeteria and shops talking to students and teachers as he moved from one area to another. This was his way of staying in touch with people.

When he became assistant superintendent of the Chattanooga Public Schools in 1972, he carried this practice with him. It was a common sight to see him "walking the halls" in the building that housed the administrative offices of the Division of Instructional Services. Every morning, he would make his rounds and talk to each person on his staff. Directors, supervisors, and secretaries would all get equal time.

He rarely telephoned anyone in the building. He preferred to talk personally with people. He thought that a face-to-face conference was more informative and productive. He believed that a person's expressions and body language gave him as much or more information than words could.

It was his practice, also, to visit each school in the system and talk with principals, teachers, staff members, and students. At that time there were 55 schools that saw him on a regular basis. Even today, years after he retired from the Chattanooga Public Schools, teachers will tell me how much they miss his visiting their classrooms and taking the time to listen to them and support their endeavors.

Thomas Peters and Nancy Austin, in *A Passion For Excellence*, refer to this leadership practice as MBWA - Management by Wandering Around. The authors state that leading is a hands-on art. They believe that as the effective administrator "wanders" among his people, at least three activities are taking place. The leader is listening, teaching, and facilitating. He or she uses this technique to keep in touch with the members of the organization, gain firsthand information, guide and direct, and impart and reinforce the values of the organization. Thus, the leader tries to enhance the performance of those with whom he comes in contact.

How do the members of the organization perceive this type of administrator? Generally, they view this leader as one who is accessible to them. Employees believe that they have some degree of input into the system since the administrator listens to them and is available to them. They feel that they are a necessary part of the organization. When employees feel valued, a positive organizational climate ultimately develops.

Thomas Peters and Robert Waterman, Jr., of the consulting firm of McKinsey and Company, studied the management techniques of 43 of America's best-run companies to find the key to successful businesses. They wanted to know why some corporations did better than others. Why were some perceived as excellent when others were thought of as only mediocre?

The results of their study were published in the highly acclaimed and well-documented *In Search of Excellence*. In this unique book on management, the authors report that excellent corporations have eight characteristics in common, one of which is the unique way they relate to people. The successful companies treat people with respect and dignity and make them feel valued and important. They think of people as partners and as members of their business family. As a result, production increases.

When commenting on the day-to-day communication that takes place among these excellent companies, the authors state, "For information exchange, informality is the norm. People really do wander around; top management is in constant contact with employees at the lowest levels (and with customers), everyone is typically on a first-name basis."

Sam Walton, of Wal-Mart fame, was an example of an excellent manager of a successful corporation. Anyone who has heard stories or read books about him knows that he believed in getting out among his "associates" as he called his employees. Sam would visit his stores and walk up and down the aisles talking and listening to the employees and showing genuine interest in what they were doing. Sam was practicing MBWA by showing and telling his employees that he cared. Because of the time that Sam spent with his employees inviting their opinions and listening to their ideas and concerns, they felt important and valued. Sam was a great wanderer.

MBWA and Effective Teachers

Let's translate this same leadership strategy— Management By Wandering Around—to the teachers in the classroom. As teachers move among their students, what specific actions can they take to convey to their students that they value and respect them?

Effective teachers recognize and speak to each student each day.

Effective teachers recognize the power of communication, not only for instructional purposes, but also to show students that they care. Many teachers stand at the entrance to their classrooms to greet each student each morning:

> "Good Morning, Sally. We missed you yesterday. I hope you're feeling better. JoAnn will let you know what lessons you missed."

> "Hi, Andy. Is that a frog in the box?"

Effective teachers set the stage for further communication by trying to involve *all* students in daily class discussions. Teachers have their own methods for ensuring that the same students are not called on all the time. One teacher wrote the students' names on index cards. Then he mixed the cards up daily and called on the student's name that appeared at the top of the deck. By the end of the day, each student had a chance to contribute his ideas to the class.

Effective teachers monitor their students as they work independently or in groups. As the teacher moves among the students and reviews the work in progress, teacher and child have additional opportunities for brief communication.

> "Josh, your answer seems to be correct. Why don't you check the math just to be sure."

> "Andrea, your first paragraph is a real attention-getter!"

> "Chris, you're on the right track. Expand that idea a little."

Effective teachers listen to students.

A large part of communication is listening. The act (or gift) of listening to children has many advantages for teachers. First of all, many potential discipline problems have been detected by just listening to students. All too often, problems that occur in the classroom began initially in the home, the community, or at the bus stop on the way to school. These problems can be diffused before they fully develop if the teacher's antennae are attuned to the climate of the classroom.

Next, listening to students helps us discover where the learning process is breaking down. Let students "think out loud" when trying to solve problems so you can detect the exact place in the process where the student is having difficulty. Then intercede at this point with good teaching strategies.

Finally, by listening to children we realize what valuable resources they are. Each student who enters your classroom has a "history" that is the result of all his experiences, interests, and beliefs. However, we must listen to our students to become aware of the specific experiences that they have.

Once, for example, I was observing a novice teacher in a fourth grade classroom. The topic was the capital city of the United States, Washington, D. C. The teacher introduced the lesson and showed some pictures of the various monuments and points of interest. Several students raised their hands periodically, but they were never recognized by the teacher.

When the period ended, I approached the students who had raised their hands during the lesson.

"Did you want to share something with the class?" I inquired.

"I wanted to tell my teacher that I went to Washington this past summer," said the girl.

"I did, too," said another, "and I've got lots of stuff to show the class."

If only the teacher had called on these students or listened to their comments during a brief class discussion. Wouldn't the other students have benefited from these firsthand experiences of their classmates?

Effective teachers make themselves available to students during the school day.

Individual teachers demonstrate their availability in different ways. Some teachers announce to their students that they will be working in their classrooms either early in the morning or after school and that they can talk individually to students at that time. Others may eat lunch with their students in the cafeteria once or twice a week, joining in the conversations and discussing the students' interests.

Sometimes teachers become more approachable to students when they spend productive and satisfying time together. When students work in small groups or special projects with a teacher, go on class field trips together, or jointly organize class events, parties or picnics, the stage is often set for better relationships between pupils and teachers.

Some of the most enjoyable times I experienced with my students were spent in preparation for holiday plays and graduation ceremonies. There was a sense of working together for a common goal as students helped each other memorize words to poems and songs and practice parts in plays. We worked hard, but we also laughed a lot and had fun working. We began to relate to each other more as *individuals,* rather than in our typical roles of principal and students. And our relationships seemed to deepen because of those special times together.

I walked into a book store not long ago and an attractive young lady came up to me and said, "Dr. Carr, do you remember me? I was one of your Saint Elmo Saints in the Christmas program at Saint Elmo." I remembered the precious fourth and fifth grade students who were in the "Saints," the singing and dancing group that I formed when I was principal of this elementary school. We hugged each other, and all the good memories suddenly came back to me.

Effective teachers involve their students in planning the curriculum.

"We are going to be learning about volcanoes during the next few days. What would *you* like to find out about volcanoes?" the teacher asked. "Let's write some of the questions we'd like to discuss on the board . . . "

In this situation, students are active participants in their own learning. They are involved in making some decisions about what they want to learn. By brainstorming the topic, the teacher can find out not only what the students would like to know but also what they already know. I believe that students become more motivated to learn when they have a voice in the content and direction of their curriculum.

Effective teachers give students choices.

Children are unique individuals. They have their own special personalities, interests, and learning styles. Effective teachers—by working closely with students— know that they are not interested in the same things in the same ways on the same days. Education for young people is not one-size-fits-all.

We must give students more opportunities to express their individuality. We must plan times when students can select topics, stories, or projects that interest them, pursue them in their own way, and choose classmates with whom they would like to work. Effective teachers recognize these needs and try to meet them.

To summarize, Management by Wandering Around is a management strategy successful teachers employ. Note that the operative word is *wandering*.

No one can motivate or lead a class full of energetic, curious, creative students by sitting behind a desk. The teacher has to be moving among his or her students, guiding and teaching, listening and questioning, sharing and encouraging.

Walk Like You Talk

The saying, "Do as I say and not as I do" does not work with children. They are strictly "monkey see, monkey do" people and learn by imitating and mimicking the adults that are closest to them.

As adults, our actions and behavior send out louder signals than what we say. Actions really do speak louder than words. Therefore, it is important that our actions and behavior are congruent. If we say one thing and do another, we will send forth mixed signals.

Let's look at some examples of confusing signals in the classroom. Place yourself in the third desk from the front. What signals would you be receiving from the following examples?

Mrs. Robinson told the third graders that there would be "no eating or drinking in the classroom." She asked the students to write the rule in their notebooks so they wouldn't forget.

On the second day of school, Mrs. Robinson came to class carrying a cup of coffee and began to write an assignment on the board. The third graders looked at each other, then at Mrs. Robinson, and shrugged their shoulders in confusion.

In another school, Mr. Baker, the sixth grade teacher, told his students that he didn't mind quiet talking in the classroom, but there was to be "ABSOLUTELY NO TALKING" in the halls.

The next morning, when the students were going to their first class, they saw Mr. Baker standing in the halls with his co-workers, laughing loudly at a story another teacher was telling the group.

At Jones Elementary School, the staff and students decided to designate 15 minutes every afternoon as a "Read-In." All members of the school—teachers, students, the custodian and school secretary—agreed to stop what they were doing at that time to read for 15 minutes.

During the "Read-In" last Friday, Mary and Cathy looked up from their books to see Mrs. Abernathy busily recording spelling grades in her grade book. They looked at each other in disbelief.

Mixed signals are being sent out by the teachers in these examples. Rules and policies should be meant for everyone—students and teachers alike. If teachers are not following the rules, students might assume rules are not important and could possibly follow suit.

Students will lose respect for the teachers, the rules, and, in some cases, both of these.

Effective managers are particularly aware of the messages their behavior sends forth. They want their signals to be clear, easily understood, and to emphasize the values that they hold. If a teacher or principal, for example, leans down to pick up a piece of trash, it signals to those watching that he or she values a clean school. If a principal's door is open to teachers and students, it signals that the principal is available to those who work there. If a teacher gives awards for perfect attendance, it shows that being at school everyday is important. If teachers and principals present Honor or Star Roll awards, it demonstrates that they value academic achievement.

Effective managers lead by the things they give their time and attention to and by the words they say. *Being a good role model is the best way to teach.*

Successful Principals Speak Out

A few years ago, I asked successful elementary, middle, and high school principals to share one thing that helped them become more effective as administrators. The following topics were mentioned the most. Listen to the principals' own words as they talk about their multifaceted role.

Dimensions of the Principalship

Being highly visible in the school

The majority of principals believed being visible was a *must* for their leadership role to be effective.

> *I am always highly visible to the students in hallways, classrooms, and at extracurricular activities.*

> *I want the children to see me and know that I am there for them.*

> *I make it a point to smile and say 'hello'
> to every staff member every day.*

Modeling the behavior that you expect of others

> *Modeling should occur in our
> interactions with the children, parents,
> and the teachers themselves.*

> *I am out in the school modeling interest
> and involvement in the school and
> programs, and care and concern for the
> children and adults.*

Being accessible to members of the school

> *I believe in having an open door policy
> so that teachers and parents will have
> someone to listen to their concerns and
> successes.*

> *My door is always open so both kids
> and grown-ups know I'm there for them.*

Sharing decision-making with teachers, parents, and students

> *I invite the staff members to give their
> viewpoints so we can factor these in to
> arrive at a solution we can live with.*

> *If the decision affects the individuals in
> the school, they need to be involved in
> the process.*

> *I try to get everyone involved - students,
> teachers, and parents.*

Placing people first

People are my priority! I always deal with people first and paper second. This applies especially to children. This makes for long days and even longer weekends with work to do, but I believe it helps to more effectively serve my children.

I get to know each child on an individual, first name basis.

I believe that kids are my business, my top priority.

Listening

It's important to listen to all sides of a conflict or concern.

Being a good listener is the key to solving problems. Be sure to get the various perspectives before making a decision.

Listen carefully to problems and don't overreact.

Being fair

Fairness can be the key to open many doors.

When individuals know you will be fair, it goes a long way in establishing good relationships.

Keeping current with subject matter

I either teach or participate in at least one class in each subject area, including music and home economics.

I make it a point to get in the classrooms daily.

It's imperative to review the teachers' plans, sit in on grade-level meetings, and visit the classrooms often in order to stay abreast of the instructional program.

Focusing on the positive

All individuals respond to positive recognition! Good papers, appropriate behavior, good deeds, perfect attendance, and a host of other things can be used to recognize the children in your school. And don't forget the teachers! The same list and more could be used with teachers as well.

We recognize our teachers with a trophy that is circulated among the staff. It is used to recognize a variety of accomplishments of staff members - a super lesson, going the extra mile with a child or parent, volunteering for extra projects, and so on.

Recognize students for the things they are doing right. I am always looking for students who are showing kindness toward others or who are trying to keep the school neat and clean. I honor these students with good citizenship or super kid awards.

Tips for New Principals

These same principals were asked to give one tip that they would like to pass on to new or prospective principals. These are their valuable suggestions:

Be willing to work long and hard hours. Understand from the beginning that your work is never 'finished.'

Set goals; be visionary.

Understand that your primary responsibility is to enhance student learning. You are the instructional leader.

Invite community people, board members, and district office personnel to see the good things going on in your school.

Promptly follow up recommendations, concerns, or complaints. Don't put these off, because they don't go away!

Have a tough skin. Don't take things personally.

Be true to your goals and priorities. Never try to please everyone.

Find another successful veteran principal and establish a network for support and advice with that individual.

Spend time each day with students. And always keep your school student-centered.

Be flexible. Be able to shift gears.

Develop a sense of humor. You'll need it!

Turn people on by being positive yourself.

Never lose sight of the tremendously difficult tasks teachers face daily. Sometimes, because the principalship is so all-consuming, we don't take time to interact with the people with whom we are expected to lead. Teachers, students, and parents need that personal attention.

Always keep the students' welfare and education as your top priority.

I Haven't Done
Anything Today . . .

Principals often get frustrated because they feel that they never seem to get anything done. I usually make a "To Do" list and check things off as I finish them. Today's list, for example, includes two surveys from the superintendent that I must complete, an unfinished list of goals and objectives urgently requested by my area director, a growing stack of paperwork on various topics and in various stages of disarray, several letters to be answered, and a few phone calls to make.

My plan, however, does not always work. Other things somehow take precedence over the items on my list. Priorities seem to change as I go through my day. Take today, for example, when I . . .

. . . visited students in a fifth grade classroom to see how their latest science project was coming along;

. . . placed a BAND-AID® on a first grader on a scratch I couldn't see and dried away her tears by giving her a jellybean to make everything better;

. . . stopped a possible fight by appealing to the best interests of two boys by persuading them that their behavior would disappoint me if they persisted;

. . . conferred with the social worker about a student who was having difficulties in school because of home problems;

. . . took over a fourth grade teacher's classroom so she could call the nursing home to inquire about her father;

. . . consoled a parent who had lost his job and was afraid he'd have to move and transfer his children to another school;

. . . talked to a teacher about her new reading program;

. . . had lunch in the cafeteria with the six winners of the essay contest;

. . . covered the phone for the secretary so she could eat a regular lunch, instead of her usual cold drink and candy bar;

. . . read a chapter from *Charlotte's Web*
to a third grade class after they
returned from lunch;

. . . washed and dried the blue jeans of
a kindergarten child after he
experienced an "accident" and didn't
want his classmates to know;

. . . wrote a note to a new teacher on
the staff commending her for the way
she sent happy notes home with her
students;

. . . spent over an hour taking
individual pictures of Honor and Star
Roll students for a bulletin board in the
entrance hall;

. . . scheduled a field-trip to a children's
opera for our second grade students.

It's 3:00 P.M. and the school day is almost over.
I look at my list and realize that I haven't accomplished
anything on it. I decide to close my office door and
complete the list of goals and objectives requested by
my director, so I don't have to take it home with me.
As I open the folder that contains the unfinished
surveys and incomplete goals, there is a knock at my
door.

"Come in," I respond.

The door partially opens and a first grade head peeks in. "Mrs. Dr. Carr, would you listen to me read before I go home?" he asks, as he holds up his new book.

I close the folder, place it in my canvas tote bag to take home, and answer, "Of course, Jamie. I'd love to. Come and sit beside me on the sofa."

My Favorite Teacher

Cousin Matt
by
Dr. C. C. Bond

I have been fortunate to have many outstanding teachers during my student days in elementary, high school, college, and graduate school. They have all made contributions to whatever success I have achieved.

One teacher who stands out in my memory above all others as being very special is Mrs. Mattye Tollette Bond. She taught me in elementary and high school. I called her Cousin Matt because she was married to my father's first cousin, Professor Ollie S. Bond, who was also a great teacher.

Cousin Matt was a great teacher because of the following reasons:

- *She respected the worth and dignity of all of her students.*

- *She was an outstanding scholar in all the disciplines she taught (math, history, English, and foreign languages).*

- *She could challenge each student to perform at his or her highest potential.*

- *She possessed love and compassion and understanding for students who experienced difficulty and needed help and encouragement.*

- *When all else failed, she had the unique ability to keep hopes alive.*

From a personal viewpoint, she was the one who helped me most during my 11th grade year, when I had the misfortune to lose both my father and my brother, and I was forced to drop out of school. With the encouragement of my dear Mother and Cousin Matt, I re-entered school and graduated with my class in spite of my many traumatic experiences. It was her counseling and interest in me that caused me to go to college and graduate on time. This made all the difference in my life.

Cousin Matt left Brownsville and retired from teaching in New York City. She is now in reasonably good health and plans to come to Brownsville, Tennessee, to join friends, relatives, and former students to help celebrate her 100th birthday this year. I give a lot of people credit for bringing her into my life, but I give God the glory.

Part VI

ACCENTUATING THE POSITIVE

A Look at School Climate

Developing a
Positive School Climate

All organizations have a climate. Some, however, are more positive and effective than others. There are many definitions that describe climate, but generally, climate involves the perceptions people hold about an organization.

The school's organizational climate is its atmosphere for learning. It includes the feelings people have about the school and whether they believe it is a place where learning can occur. It reflects the perceptions members of the school hold in relation to their expectations of what the school should be like and how people within it should be treated. The climate mirrors the collection of attitudes, beliefs, and behaviors within the school that affect achievement.

From the moment we enter a school, we begin to receive vibes as to what the school is all about. Is the school's mission statement posted in the entrance hall?

Is the secretary friendly and helpful? Are the teachers and support personnel warm and caring with the students?   Is the school neat, orderly, and work-oriented?   Is the environment student-centered?   Is student classwork proudly displayed?   Are high expectations the norm?

As we look around the school, we gain clues as to what this school values and how this organization treats the individuals who belong there.   We begin to gain either positive or negative perceptions about the school's atmosphere for teaching and learning.

How Can Teachers Help Build A Positive School Climate?

The climate of the classroom affects the way the students live and learn. Classroom teachers shared the following suggestions for creating a positive learning environment:

Treat all students with respect and courtesy.

Hold high expectations for all students.

Teach children to look for the good in themselves and in their work.

Too often students who have a poor self image are severely critical of their own work. Help children build a healthy image by looking for the things that they do right.

"Look at your papers," said the teacher. "What are the best parts of them?"

Some of the students' responses were: "My writing is getting better," "The ending to my story is funny," and "My paper is neat."

Teach children to look for the good in others.
A group of third grade teachers designed a bulletin board for their wing of the school that said, "Good Things Are Happening Here!" Students were asked to write notes describing the good things they observed other students and personnel doing.

Let's look at some of the notes displayed on the bulletin board:

> "Today I saw Mary empty the pencil sharpener without being asked."

> "Fred helped Andrew study for his spelling test."

> "Marie picked up papers that Mrs. Tindell dropped."

> "Mr. Russell, the head custodian, helped Joseph carry the books."

Students found that by concentrating on the positive things happening around them, they had less time or inclination to dwell on negative occurrences.

Recognize students for their progress and improvements.
Designating a "pride wall" for displaying achievement certificates, special awards, and good work is an excellent way to recognize the students for the accomplishments they are making in the classroom.

Use various teaching strategies in your classroom so students who learn in different ways have a better opportunity to succeed.

Good teachers use a variety of methods and media to make learning more interesting.   Children need visuals and hands-on experiences.   They need to work in groups and with partners, as well as independently.

Inform students and parents of mid-grading period progress so parents and students will have an opportunity to improve any below average grades.   Give kids a "second chance" if they fail to bring in homework or don't do well on a test.

Our purpose is to help children achieve, not fail. We want to give them every opportunity to succeed.

Refrain from discussing students negatively in the faculty lounge or other school areas.

Remember that the students are *your* students and their problems should be held in confidence.

Involve students in the managing and operation of the daily classroom duties.

Throw out the red grading pen.   Focus more on what the students are doing right.

Smile and enjoy your students.

Promote your classroom and school as "a good place to be."

How Can Principals Help Promote A Good School Climate?

A good school climate does not just happen. It is a collaborative effort of teachers, support personnel, students, parents, and principals. The following are some methods and activities that principals employ to create and maintain good learning environments.

Promote pride in the school.

Begin by examining the building in which learning will take place. Clean up! Fix up! Spruce up! A coat of paint, a new pair of curtains, a colorful bulletin board can be the beginning steps to transform a drab school to a dazzling one. When a school is neat, clean, and colorful, teachers and students alike have more pride in it.

Value instructional time.

Signal to teachers that you value instruction. Designate a large block of instructional time as "sacred." During this time, refrain from interrupting teachers with public address announcements, assemblies, or other noninstructional classroom disturbances.

Provide time for planning together.

Schedule time for teachers to share and plan together. Weekly grade-level meetings or departmental planning sessions promote interaction among faculty members. These times of togetherness can contribute to developing and strengthening the bonds necessary for a strong positive climate.

Keep the members of the school informed.

Keep the faculty, students, and parents informed about what is going on in the school. Many schools distribute a weekly newsletter announcing upcoming events. One principal wrote a daily bulletin for her staff members. She included the day's agenda and recognized various teachers for the unique or good things she observed happening in their classrooms.

Celebrate academic successes.

Encourage assemblies, ceremonies, and rituals that celebrate academic successes and instructional improvements. Honor teachers and students who contribute to improving the quality of life in the school.

One principal has a giant fish bowl in the hall. The names of all students who achieve honor, star, or most improved status are placed in the bowl, and each grading period the principal *goes fishing* for the lucky prize winners.

Share decision-making with others.

Involve teachers and other staff members in decision-making processes, especially if the results directly affect them. Everyone in the school should be expected to take a cooperative responsibility for what happens in the school. Through shared decision-making, members of the school gain a sense of ownership and pride in the school and its programs.

Tell and retell good school stories.

Take every opportunity to tell and retell stories that demonstrate that your school is unique or special. Good stories convey meanings about what your school is all about.

When I was principal of Saint Elmo Elementary School, our logo was a picture of a little saint with a lopsided halo tilted over one side of his head. We placed this symbol on school stationary, invitations, handbooks, and newsletters. Our students loved to tell the story of our school logo which symbolized that we were continually working to move toward excellence: "We're Saint Elmo Saints. We have crooked halos because we are not quite perfect yet, but that's okay, 'cause *we're always trying!"*

Get involved with your students.

When principals give their time and attention to students, they signal that students are important. Visit classrooms frequently and comment on students' work. Display students' papers in your office and in the main halls. One principal gives a "POP" award to students who show exceptional progress. The students love to receive this "**P**ride **o**f the **P**rincipal" certificate because it has a *tootsie pop* taped to it.

Another principal has a "treasure chest" in his office. He invites students honored as Honor, Star Roll, and Most Improved to select a prize from the treasure chest. The principal reported that "many times the kids pick something from the chest for their mothers."

One elementary principal has a "principal's brag strip" in the front hall where she posts the students' art work, creative writing, and exceptional papers. She says the children "really love the attention they get from other people bragging on their work."

Some principals take pictures of students who have achieved special status. These pictures are displayed in the entrance hall for all to enjoy.

Many principals plan special events for their high-achieving students. A middle school principal sponsors a "principal's superstars" field trip each grading period. Picnics on the school grounds, movies, popcorn parties, and trips to local museums or aquariums are favorite activities for recognizing outstanding students.

One principal schedules a "lunch with the principal" each six weeks. Students selected by the teachers for special achievements are invited to dine with the principal.

Principals report that they are increasingly including students in the planning and implementation of the school's goals and programs. Students are being placed on discipline, cafeteria, and safety committees. By involving students, principals display a genuine interest in the value of students' ideas and achievements.

Principals are in a key position to affect change in schools, not necessarily because of their administrative authority, but because they are part of the setting where change will evolve. In schools, as in any organization, real changes can occur only from within. When teachers and principals make students and their instructional program the number one priority, the school's climate becomes a strong positive entity.

What Should A Good School Climate Convey To Parents?

The environment should convey the feeling that the school is a place where parents are always welcome.

Many schools display a "Welcome Parents" banner in the entrance hall. What a great feeling for the parents when they see this upon entering the building!

The school secretary is probably the most important person in the school when it comes to parents. The secretary is usually the first person the parent meets when entering the school and the person with whom the parent generally communicates when Johnny is going to be late or needs to be picked up early for a doctor's appointment. Therefore, the secretary is a key figure in establishing good public relations between the school and home.

Don't leave this task, however, entirely to the secretary. Each member of the school has a role in public relations. In my visits to schools, I notice how schools welcome visitors. A smile or "good morning" by students and teachers means so much.

Parents feel more welcomed in the school when personnel make it easy for parents to find their way around the building. Most schools ask parents to sign in at the office where the secretary can assist them with a problem or give directions to a particular classroom or area. Some schools display a school map for parents in the office or entrance hall and post room numbers and names of teachers on the outside of classroom doors.

Many schools have a parent room where parents can hang their coats and have a cup of coffee before going to the classrooms. Parents can use this room for meetings or as a workroom when helping with school projects.

Well-informed parents tend to be more positive about the school, so the school should set up avenues of communication to inform parents about school functions and invite them to be a part of the educational program.

You can get an A+ with parents if you:

- Distribute school calendars containing dates of important school events.

- Send out class newsletters announcing the good things that are happening in the classroom and explaining how parents can assist.

- Spotlight in the school newspaper parents who contribute to school activities.

- Include parents on invitation lists for Open Houses, holiday programs, American Education Week, and graduation ceremonies.

- Periodically, send flyers to parents outlining test-taking tips for students, ways parents can volunteer in the schools, recommended books for the summer reading program, and other topics of interest to parents.

The climate should communicate to parents that they are valued and needed.

Many schools have a parent bulletin board where pictures are displayed of parents involved in various school events. When parents see other parents actively contributing to the school and recognized for their efforts, they are more inclined to become involved themselves.

Parent Appreciation Days are celebrated in many schools at the end of the school year. Volunteers are given awards for assisting the school.

The climate should invite parents to become partners with teachers, have input into the goals and expectations of the school, and participate in decision-making processes.

Parents are no longer thought of as cookie-bakers or party-makers. Parents are taking an active role in the future of their children. More and more, parents are joining administrators in making decisions about budgets, school construction and maintenance, personnel, and instructional programs.

Children are profoundly influenced by the way home and school interact. Students perform better in a climate where parents and teachers support each other. Some schools feel so strongly about the positive effects of parent involvement that they ask parents to sign a contract pledging to assist in the schools for a designated number of hours each month.

The perceptions parents hold about schools are powerful and long-lasting and are formed in part by the way parents and teachers work together to create a better educational climate. In addition, the bond between parents and school is often strengthened by the small everyday acts performed for children by caring teachers. The following story demonstrates that little things really do mean a lot:

A teacher in my school had a commendable practice of calling one of her student's parents each night to comment about how the student was progressing in class. One morning a parent met me in the hall before school and said, "Josh's teacher called me last night. She wanted to remind me to tell Josh that there was a program about dinosaurs on educational TV. She knew Josh loved anything about dinosaurs, and she didn't want him to miss it!" She paused, and then added, "Can you believe she took her own personal time to call about the program? She's a great teacher, you know, so thoughtful. We really love this school."

Recipe for
A Positive Classroom

Mix the following "measurable" items and season them to your taste. Remember that this recipe does not have to be followed to the letter. You will want to add more than a dash of love and spice it up with your own personality and style. Blend well and shape into a positive classroom.

- A teacher who smiles, likes students, and enjoys teaching

- Students who respect themselves, others, and others' property

- Parents who enjoy participating in classroom activities

- A principal who visits the classroom and celebrates the learning taking place there

- Learning and library areas that are inviting, attractive, and motivating

- Bulletin boards that display *all* students' best work

- A teacher who gives each student at least one positive comment daily

- Students who actively participate in their own learning

- Students who assume daily responsibilities for the school and have a personal stake in its success

School-*Wise* Instructions

The wise old owl that usually circles over only the very best and most effective schools and notices everything that goes on in them has these words of wisdom for all of us . . .

Treat each child in your room as if he or she were your own.

Have a positive comment for each student each day. Remember, everyone (even this ol' owl) needs to be noticed and appreciated.

Wear a smile. A positive, friendly, helpful attitude will take you far.

Always pull your weight in school projects. It is easier to multiply success when you divide the tasks.

Try to do something thoughtful for at least one fellow teacher each day. A brief note in a teacher's box may "make his day" and it is guaranteed to make yours!

Share your materials and good teaching ideas with others. It's not nice to be a miser.

Always leave home problems where they belong- at home.

Make it a rule to clean up your own mess and teach your students to follow your example.

Strike an attentive pose in faculty meetings, even if for no other reason than to make your principal happy.

Learn how to make a special dessert for faculty functions. It's the best way to win friends and influence appetites.

Always be punctual. And expect this quality in others.

Remember that little children are not as fragile as you think. They can be hugged, loved, and patted with very little permanent damage done to them.

Learn to listen—especially to children and more experienced teachers.

You don't have to raise your voice to show authority. Those who are truly in control can whisper and command attention.

Learn from younger teachers, for they bring fresh ideas and new approaches to the field of education.

Learn from older teachers, for age and experience often mix to give them wisdom.

Give a word of encouragement to the custodian, the secretary, the support personnel, and the cafeteria staff, for they are valuable members of the school team.

Try to understand that no one is all knowing, completely right, or always perfect (except this wise ol' owl, of course!) This will help you have compassion for others and will certainly curtail any personal guilt trips you may have about your own insecurities.

Accept each child who enters your room as one who has a clean slate. Don't be *too* quick to review his school records.

There will always be rainy Mondays when someone has your parking space, the coffee pot is on the blink, the toilet won't flush, your students stare at you blankly while you are explaining their assignments, and you are late for the faculty meeting. But remember, there is always tomorrow . . . *thank goodness!*

All professions have their tricks of the trade. In your bag of tricks, include the following: safety pins, a few sharpened pencils, some special treats for a job well done, lots of compassion and empathy, and a generous portion of love.

Teaching can be an extremely isolated profession, and it will remain so until teachers reach out to each other to form the bonds that will enrich their personal and professional lives. Reach out today.

Periodically, do something nice for someone in secret. The recipient won't know who to thank, but *you* will.

Lead a balanced life—some work, some play, some rest, some prayer—and just some time to reflect. There is more to your life than school.

Always try to leave your world—your room, school, and community—better than you found it.

School life is full of ups and downs, joys and disappointments, successes and failures. Accept them all with dignity and compassion.

You'll find that you don't have to call the role. It's so much easier to just look around the classroom and *count your blessings!*

❦❦❦   *My Favorite Teacher*   ❦❦❦

The Legacy
by
Marcia Kling

My life has been profoundly influenced by the teachers I had growing up in New York's Westchester County. To an extent, the time in which I came along was a factor in the depth of that influence. It was a time when teachers were highly regarded, and I believed most of mine to be the epitome of everything wise and wonderful!

Then, too, my own father's involvement in education set the tone for my perception. Classically educated in Europe as well as in this country, my dad could have done almost anything he wished. But Roger Hoyt Williams genuinely enjoyed young people and wanted to share with them his love of language and literature and so began his career as a teacher of English on the high school level.

After a stint as acting superintendent of schools during the Second World War, he returned to the high school as principal. To this day, when I'm with people who attended school under him, they speak of my father with great fondness and appreciation for his fairness and concern for their well-being. It's a mark of the depth of that interest, I think, that until the day he died he remembered the names of almost every student who ever attended Peekskill High School and followed their lives with real pride. (I think it would please him very much that one of his students became the governor of New York State!)

*   *   *   *   *

Perhaps the most profound personal influence in my life, though, was exerted by Laura Ackerman, who taught second grade. Miss Ackerman was absolutely dedicated to her profession and to her young charges. Many of her students were from families newly arrived in this country, with little experience in the democratic process. To develop her students' understanding of and appreciation for good citizenship, she modeled her classroom after the U. S. government, from the president on down.

The year I had Miss Ackerman, I was fortunate enough to be chosen class president. What a responsibility to assume at the ripe age of seven! But what a great learning experience! To this day, I remember the lessons learned about fairness and honestly and the importance of every person doing his part to make government—in EVERY setting—work.

A tragic classroom accident cut short Miss Ackerman's teaching career, but it did nothing to diminish her interest in the students she'd had over the years. Until she died many years later, I received a greeting on every occasion and a note of pride for every achievement. And I was not the only one, by any means.

In my opinion, that kind of genuine interest and encouragement is the gift every teacher owes her students. The payoff is inestimable, to the student, the educator, the system, and ultimately, our world.

Part VII

Introducing...
Me!

*Presenting
Yourself in the
Best Possible Way*

HELP WANTED: MALE/FEMALE

An individual who has a love for children, works well with people, is willing to "go the extra mile" and has a passion for teaching and learning. Must also possess the qualities of the following:

NURSE	CONSULTANT
PSYCHOLOGIST	ARTIST
COUNSELOR	ACTOR
SOCIAL WORKER	ACCOUNTANT
FACILITATOR	BOOKKEEPER
INSTRUCTOR	CATERER
SECRETARY	DECORATOR
TOUR GUIDE	FUND RAISER
MEDIATOR, JUDGE	SALESPERSON
MUSICAL DIRECTOR	PUBLIC RELATIONS
CHOREOGRAPHER	EXPERT

Clock watchers need not apply.

The Interview

You finally have an interview! After weeks and weeks of completing application forms and securing quality references, you have your first interview session scheduled. You are both excited and nervous. Questions begin to flood your mind. What should I wear? What questions will I be asked? How can I prepare? What if I'm rejected?

Keep in mind that the interview is a two-way street; it is not an inquisition. It is an opportunity for the interviewer and the applicant to meet and exchange information in order to decide if a good match exists between the individual and the organization.

You should not be intimidated by this process. On the other hand, you shouldn't be too relaxed about this very important event. In order to have a successful meeting, planning is crucial.

This chapter is for student teachers who are preparing for their first interview and for teachers who are either applying for new positions or reentering the profession after a period of absence. It is intended to allay the fears associated with this procedure and help the prospective applicant prepare for this special event.

Although procedures and specifics will vary in different school systems, a common thread of applicant expectations and interview questions prevail. This chapter includes practical tips for a successful interview, suggestions about videotapes and portfolios, and interview questions that the applicant will want to consider. It concludes with the qualities administrators look for when interviewing prospective staff members.

General Tips Before the Interview

Advance Planning

The success of a job interview begins long before the meeting takes place. Preparation is the key. Prepare by having your portfolio or samples of your work ready, deciding what you will wear to the interview, learning about the school that has the vacancy, and practicing answers to anticipated interview questions.

Know your interviewer's name and title. If you are not sure, call his or her secretary and ask. You do not want to make the mistake of addressing a person by the incorrect title.

Plan to arrive on the premises five to ten minutes early. Allow yourself enough time in case of unexpected delays. By arriving a little early, you will have a few minutes to catch your breath and collect your thoughts.

Be courteous and positive with everyone in the reception offices. Remember that from the minute you walk in, everyone is forming an opinion of you which you want to be favorable.

Have your portfolio or other samples of achievements, experiences, and honors available should you be asked to share them with the interviewer.

Carry a small notebook and pen with you. Do not take notes during the interview, but if you are given dates to remember, you will have some place to record them.

Dressing For The Interview

Part of your advance planning is deciding what to wear to the interview. It is best to select clothes that are on the conservative side. You want to appear businesslike and professional. Please, no fads in fashion, and ladies, no jingles, jangles, or dangles in jewelry!

A Dress Rehearsal . . .

Have a "dress rehearsal" before the big day. Dress in your entire outfit (undergarments, accessories, shoes, everything!) and stand in front of a full-length mirror. Check it all out, both back and front. Next, sit in a chair in front of the mirror. Does anything "ride up" where it shouldn't? Does the outfit wrinkle too easily? If you notice any problems, you still have time to change your attire or make necessary corrections. If everything looks the way you want it to, then hang up the outfit and you'll be ready to go.

"Remove One Accessory" Rule . . .

Many women have a tendency to wear too many accessories. As a rule of thumb, you'll look better if you will remove one accessory (bracelet, necklace, pin) from your outfit.

The Value of First Impressions . . .

One cannot emphasize enough the importance of first impressions for they tend to color the rest of the interview. A person who arrives late will have the difficult, if not impossible, task of trying to regain the interviewer's confidence. A person who appears disorganized or acts in an unprofessional manner will more than likely not be considered for the position. Therefore, remember the **"3 P's of Interviewing"**:

> **Always be . . .**
> **P**repared,
> **P**unctual, and
> **P**rofessional.

Remember, you only get one chance to make a good first impression!

During the Interview

If you have a choice of where to sit, choose the chair closest to the interviewer. A straight-backed chair is better than a comfortable sofa. This is not the time to sink into the cushions of a sofa and become permanently wedged there.

If you are offered coffee, it's probably best to decline gracefully. It is terribly difficult to balance a cup of coffee and your portfolio at the same time.

Make a personal observation about the interviewer or his or her office. Be sincere.

> "Oh, I see that you are a graduate of Vanderbilt. My brother graduated from there."

> "That painting of children over your desk is one of my favorites. It's so realistic."

Display an attitude of enthusiasm throughout the interview to show the interviewer you really want to work for the organization.

Please, no mannerisms! A personnel director in a nearby school system stated that nervous mannerisms are terribly distracting. She recalled one applicant who "twirled" a strand of hair during the entire interview, another who repeatedly brushed off the shoulders of his suit coat, and still another who kept tugging at the hem of her dress.

Don't get involved in discussing any controversial issues. If the school system is getting ready to elect board members or become consolidated, stay away from those subjects.

Answering Questions . . .

In order to answer any questions intelligently, you must know yourself and your skills. Prior to the interview, make an inventory of your goals, skills, honors and achievements, and know how to communicate them to the interviewer.

If a question is confusing or ambiguous, ask for a clarification. Pause to collect your thoughts before answering. Do not rush your answers. Take your time.

Match your answer to the question. If the question is a broad one dealing with concepts, answer it in general terms. But if the interviewer is asking for specifics, then be *specific*.

Look at the person when you are talking. However, don't get hung up on this. You want to appear natural and talk conversationally.

Remember I stated previously that an interview is a two-way street. You, too, will have inquiries about the position. If you have any specific questions about the school or your classroom, this is the time to ask them.

At the Close of the Interview . . .

Thank the interviewer for the time spent with you. Be positive and smile.

More than likely, he or she has many other candidates to consider before a decision can be made, so you cannot expect an answer immediately. However, if the job is appealing, you might want to conclude by saying, "I really like this school, and I'd love to be a part of its staff. I hope you will consider me seriously for this position."

After the Interview

H. Anthony Medley, in his delightful and informative book entitled *Sweaty Palms: The Neglected Art of Being Interviewed*, suggests that the individual should write a synopsis of each interview immediately following it. He says this is extremely helpful when the person has many different appointments and the particulars of each could become confusing over time.

Medley recommends that you record exactly what occurred, what was said, and your impression of the interviewer and the position. This information may assist you later in making a choice concerning these jobs.

A Thank You Note . . .

Before you can consider that the interview is concluded, you need to extend a basic courtesy to the interviewer by sending a thank you note stating your appreciation for the time given you.

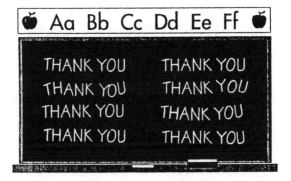

Interview Questions

I interviewed elementary principals in various school systems to find out what questions and strategies they used when interviewing prospective teachers. Many of their questions focused on the applicant's professional goals and aspirations, strengths and weaknesses, instructional strategies, discipline philosophy, and knowledge of children.

The principals agreed that the applicants' *specific* answers to questions were not as important as the manner in which they were answered. They wanted applicants who were organized in their thinking, articulate, enthusiastic, and confident.

Sample Questions

The following pages contain some examples of questions that these administrators shared with me.

Tell me about yourself (or some type of "warm up" question to get the interview started). This is a great opportunity to tell about your strengths, achievements, and qualifications, and why you want this particular job.

Why do you want to be a teacher? If the applicant is an experienced teacher who is seeking another position, the following question might be asked: *"Why do you think you would be the best qualified person for this position?"*

What special talents, hobbies, or personal qualities do you have that would add to our school program?

What are your beliefs about disciplining students?

What interesting articles or books have you read lately about teaching?

What approach would you use to teach math or science?

How would you help develop a more positive self-image in a student?

How do you plan to provide for students with individual differences in a classroom with various learning styles and levels?

What strengths/weaknesses do you have? Suggestion: If asked about a weakness, do not state a weakness that can be perceived as a strength: "I am just too organized" or "I am a perfectionist!" Good interviewers are aware of this tactic and do not buy it. It would be better to honestly state an area with which you need some help and tell the specific steps you are taking to improve in this area.

Written Responses to Questions

Many principals ask the prospective teacher to *write* the answers to several questions. The principal then has a sample of the applicant's command of the English language and how the teacher organizes his or her thoughts. In addition, the answers to these questions often become the springboard for further discussion. Some examples of these questions are, as follows:

Describe a typical morning in your classroom.

Describe your new classroom. (Include the students' seating arrangement, the location of the teacher's desk, any learning centers, study areas, or points of interest.)

How would you describe your teaching style?

How would you explain your plan for encouraging more parents to become involved in your classroom?

Think about a teacher who had a good influence on your life. List, in order of importance, five admirable qualities of that teacher.

You may have some open-ended statements to complete:

I believe children _____.

I think this school _____.

As a teacher, I _____.

I want to work (where? with whom?)

_____.

Education should _____.

Many questions, both oral and written, may be placed in the context of school problems to be solved. The following are some examples of these:

You are in the middle of teaching a lesson. One student becomes angry, storms from the room, and slams the door after him. How would you handle this situation?

It is the first day of school, and you have your hands full helping your students get settled in their new environment. A parent of one of your

students knocks at the door and asks
to talk to you about a problem his child
is having. How would you handle this
situation?

Team Approach

Many schools use the "team approach" when
interviewing prospective teachers. The team usually
consists of the grade-level chairperson and several
teachers from the school staff. Although the process
can be carried out in various ways, the teachers usually
interview the candidates, rate them in specific
categories, and submit their top two or three choices
to the principal. The principal and assistant principal
then interview the top candidates and submit their final
recommendations for the position to the personnel
department.

Video Tapes

Some school systems are suggesting or even requiring that candidates for teaching positions include a videotape of a sample of their teaching with the application. If this is required of you, the following are a few suggestions you might like to consider.

Begin the tape by introducing yourself and providing a brief description of your class and the topic and context of the lesson you will be teaching. This introduction to the lesson should take about two or three minutes and can be taped in advance.

The taping of the lesson should be continuous and unedited, showing the teacher interacting with his or her students in the classroom. Teachers who use a tripod to steady their recorder while taping this section usually produce the best results. Avoid close-ups of the students, as it is important to protect the students' right to privacy. Many schools ask parents to sign a release form for permission to videotape their children.

A written lesson plan including the topic, objectives, materials, instructional activities, and evaluation strategies should accompany the tape. Keep the lesson simple and focused on the objectives.

Some individuals conclude the tape with a brief analysis of the lesson addressing the areas they liked most, what they learned from teaching the lesson, what changes they would make if they were to reteach the lesson, and what activities the class did as a follow-up. Always end your presentation on a positive note.

Portfolios

Many universities and colleges require prospective teachers to develop portfolios which summarize their student teaching experiences. The portfolio is viewed as a reflection of the student's potential as a future employee. It should demonstrate that the student is organized, creative, neat, competent, and professional. It should be attractive and inviting so the interviewer will want to review it.

Universities have various requirements concerning the contents of the portfolio. Generally, however, they contain the following broad topics:

- **Information About the Candidate**
  Résumé
  Student's Philosophy of Education
  Official University Transcript

- **Placement Descriptions of the Student Teacher's Experience**

- **Samples of Lesson Plans, Units, Projects**

- **Methods Used to Evaluate Academic Achievement in the Classroom**

- **Specific Management Policies, Classroom Rules and Procedures**

- **Original Teaching Materials**

- **Professional Activities, Meetings, and Achievements**

- **Copies of the Student Teacher's Evaluations**

Portfolios for Experienced Teachers

If you are an experienced teacher seeking a position in another system or location, you may want to develop a portfolio that will demonstrate your competency in the field of teaching. The portfolio should reflect your personality, so be as creative as you wish.

Photographs always add interest to a portfolio. Include some of your last classroom, showing your students involved in various activities and projects.

Your first section will include **demographic information** about you. Include an up-to-date résumé in this section.

You will probably want one section entitled **original teaching materials** that will contain samples or pictures of materials you have developed. Photographs of creative bulletin boards, displays, learning centers, games, field trips, or special school events are always eye-catchers.

Include a section on **professional responsibilities** to demonstrate that you are a responsible and dependable individual. Think about the various school activities in which you have been involved. Have you conducted any workshops or seminars? Were you a grade-level or departmental chairperson? Have you assisted in the planning or implementation of a faculty or parent-teacher meeting? Did you chair a committee for your school? Include any documentation you have for these activities or make a list of professional meetings or activities stating your specific role in each.

Remember that your portfolio is a personal advertisement of your achievements, so don't be shy. Include any honors or awards you received during your career.

I would advise every teacher to keep an ongoing visual record of his or her professional achievements and accomplishments. You never know when changes may occur during your career that might require a document to be used for "show and tell."

Many teachers use a large three-ring binder with plastic sheet protectors, separated into sections with tabbed dividers for this purpose. It is a good idea to review the portfolio periodically, revising, deleting, and adding materials, in order to keep it current.

Personal Qualities

Principals were asked to state qualities that they look for when interviewing prospective staff members. Listed below are the qualities that were mentioned the most:

- A well-rounded individual—one who has a variety of interests, hobbies, and talents

- A person who really cares about children, their education and well-being

- A positive person with a sense of humor

- A cooperative person who can work well with students, teachers, parents, and administrators

- Someone who will go the "extra mile" without having to be asked

- An individual who is flexible and can adjust to change

- Someone who can make subjects interesting for students

- A person who will continue to grow professionally

- A person who will fit in with the philosophy and goals of the existing staff

- An individual who will be loyal to the ideals of the school and to its staff members

Suggestions From a Principal

Many administrators in the various school systems were kind enough to assist me with this chapter on the interview process. I would like to close with some suggestions shared by a successful principal in a quality elementary school in Catoosa County, Georgia:

- Be positive. Do not speak unkindly of other educators or schools or past work experiences.

- Be aware of your posture. Lean toward the person interviewing you.

- Be sincere.

- Look at the interviewer. Speak clearly. Take your time.

- Be specific when answering questions; use examples when possible.

- Ask for clarification if you do not understand the question.

- Don't be afraid to laugh.

- PREPARE, PREPARE, PREPARE!

- Then relax and be yourself.

You now have an idea of what good administrators are looking for and how to present yourself in the best possible way. The rest is up to you!

If I Knew Then
What I Know Now

The first few years of the new teacher's career are the most crucial. It is during this time that many teachers who have unsuccessful experiences in the classroom decide to leave the profession.

I believe professionals should help and support one another. However, many new teachers seldom seek assistance from other teachers.

Experienced teachers are more than willing to give advice, encouragement, and their own time to help new teachers get started right. I asked teachers from the elementary, middle, and high school levels to offer a word of advice to new teachers. I wish these teachers had been with me when I was beginning my career.

Help/Advice/Mentoring

You are new to a very complex and demanding profession. A little help from an experienced teacher can smooth the process of learning to teach effectively.

Always have someone you can go to as a mentor.

Don't be afraid to ask questions or ask for help or advice.

Children

During the first two weeks of school, I call every parent in my room with a positive comment about their children. I tell them that I'm looking forward to a great year and see if they have anything they want to share with me. It really starts the year on a good note!

Enjoy the children. Don't be afraid to share your life with them.

Take time to get to know your students. They can be lots of fun!

Be enthusiastic about what you teach and who you teach. Like the children and let them know it.

Make sure the children know you care about them.

Instruction/Learning

Believe that all students can learn.

Learn how kids learn. If you can do that, you can be a successful teacher anywhere.

Always overplan your lessons.

Know the subject you are teaching. Don't try to wing it! Know where you are going with the lesson and know how to get there.

Have high expectations.

Create a positive atmosphere that is conducive to learning.

Classroom Management

Always be well-organized.

Make your classroom as attractive and inviting as possible. Interesting learning centers and areas for reading and independent work add a spark to the students' day.

Be prepared. Don't wait until the official opening date of school to begin working on your classroom or lessons. Get as much as possible done ahead of time so you can be ready on the first day to place your full concentration on your students.

Observe effective teachers and see what strategies they are using successfully.

Use good classroom management techniques from the very first day of school. This sets the tone for the entire year.

Be prepared to be flexible. Sometimes your schedule gets interrupted at a moment's notice. Learn to adjust and continue.

Always expect the unexpected!

Discipline

Be fair, firm, and consistent.

Encourage, promote, and reward responsible behavior from Day One. Children must learn to be responsible and independent, not only in school, but also in life.

Establish a firm discipline plan during the first week of the school year. Always involve the kids.

Respect each student as an individual.

Always find something to like about each student. It's okay to dislike behavior while still caring for that person. Do everything possible to raise the self-esteem of students having problems.

Professional Growth

Be willing to take the time it requires to be a good teacher.

Get involved with teacher organizations. They help you know what is happening in education, and you will feel more professional.

Stay abreast of current readings and research.

Subscribe to at least one professional journal.

Do one thing each year (attend a convention, take a class, conduct a workshop) that will help you grow professionally.

Personal

Have a sense of humor. It can get both you and your students through many a rough spot.

Get to know someone who can "show you the ropes."

New teachers should take time after their daily teaching schedule to do something that is not school-related. Learn to balance your life.

Stay away from gossip; it can be a tangled web!

Sometimes you will have bad days, but don't give up. It gets better, and the personal rewards of teaching are well worth it.

Use common sense and pray for guidance.

When you cease to really like the kids and teaching, get out!

My Favorite Teacher

Lighting A Candle of Hope
by
Dr. Clifford L. Hendrix, Jr.

It is not often that I have had the opportunity to visit the "west side" where I was born and grew up. However, on those rare occasions when I have found the time to ride through, I have fondly recalled the most positive experiences as a student at the James A. Henry Elementary School. Even now I remember the impact that the teachers had on my growing up.

It certainly holds true that those first years of schooling, including preschool, are most essential to the growth and development of the child. The staff at James A. Henry made an impression on me from the beginning, when I had the good fortune of entering the first grade in this brand new school on Grove Street. At the opening ceremonies, we all stood at attention around the flagpole as the flag was raised for the first time and recited the "pledge of allegiance."

I remember my principal, Mrs. Hogue, a tall, stately, grey-haired woman who distinguished herself among students as the lady who rang the "cow bell" to denote that recess had ended and it was time to "fall in line." But most of all, I remember my sixth grade teacher, Mrs. Lois Hamilton. This attractive and neatly dressed young lady gave me the confidence to believe that I could achieve and succeed. I especially remember her conducting a drill activity in the basic fundamentals of arithmetic and following with a pop quiz.

There was one student who always excelled in every subject and every grade. No one had ever made a higher grade than she, and whenever grades were announced, it was expected that she would be at the head of the class. However, on this occasion there was someone else who made the highest score. Yes, by only two points I was at the head of the class. When Mrs. Hamilton announced the grades, she gave special recognition to my achievement and to my *amazement my classmates gave their approval. From that point, I accepted the challenge to achieve to my fullest potential.*

Although I remember it with much pride, the incident in itself is insignificant. The true significance is reflected in the change that this achievement had on my attitude and confidence in my ability to excel. No doubt it was the turning point which led to my completing high school and pursuing undergraduate and graduate studies.

Finally, reliving this experience demonstrates the kind of influence that a significant adult can have on the life of a growing child. Too much emphasis is placed on the negative influence which leads to a child's destruction. Fortunately, there are more occasions now where positive influences result in the kind of awakening that lights a candle of hope in the face of darkness.

I'm thankful that this outstanding lady was concerned and cared enough to light a candle for me.

Part VIII

USING
TIME WISELY

Ways to Make
Each Moment Count

Make Each Moment Count

With today's curriculum becoming increasingly crowded, it is more important than ever for teachers to use every instructional minute. Many minutes, which could easily be lost if we're not careful, can be used for productive learning activities that increase teacher effectiveness and reinforce the students' previously developed concepts.

When do these minutes occur? Analyze your own daily schedule to determine when time might be lost. Pay particular attention to the first and last few minutes of the day and to transitional times between one lesson or subject and the next. Look at the time immediately before and after lunch and recess. When students are waiting — waiting for class to convene, waiting for materials to be passed, waiting for attendance to be taken, waiting for a turn — little learning is taking place.

Let's look at how a few lost minutes here and there can add up:

> Mrs. Jenkins tells her third grade students to sit quietly while she collects lunch money.
> (4 minutes lost)
>
> Next she passes out work for the students to complete. The students wait patiently until everyone receives a paper.   (3 minutes lost)
>
> Later, the students line up for mid-morning break. The students are asked to wait until another class finishes in the restroom.
> (3 minutes lost)

If no other time is lost that day, Mrs. Jenkins has already lost 10 minutes. It doesn't sound like much, but if you multiply this by 180 school days, it totals 1800 minutes or 30 hours. Almost a full week of instructional time has been lost.

Now let's see if we can be more creative with our use of time. In the following examples, you will note how effective teachers turn these lost minutes into instructional time.

When passing out math papers, a third grade teacher called out math facts for the students to complete orally. "I was very pleased with your math papers," she commented. "While I'm returning them to you, let's review some of the more difficult facts. What is 6 times 9, Mary? What about 8 times 7, Andrew? . . . "

A second grade teacher lined up his students for lunch only to find out that the cafeteria line was backed up. Rather than lose this time, he turned it into a constructive opportunity.

"We're going to be detained for a few minutes," he said. "While we are in line, let's have some fun! We're going to play 'categories' and name different kinds of food in alphabetical order. Laurie, you begin with A."

"Applesauce," said Laurie.
"Keep it going, Richard," said the teacher.
"Barbecue!" chimes in Richard.

These short activities requiring little or no preparation or materials give students the opportunity to review, practice, and apply familiar skills. I call these *5-Minute Activities* because they fill short periods of time that might otherwise be lost.

On the following pages are additional examples of *5-Minute Activities.* Most can be adapted to any skill you have previously covered with your class. No resource credits were attempted since I collected the majority of these activities over a period of twenty-five years from ideas gained from sources ranging from the practical experiences of classroom teachers to examples outlined in various workshops, seminars, and educational books and journals.

I sincerely hope that you and your students profit from the use of *5-Minute Activities.* You will find that you can easily change waiting time into solid instructional time. Time is so precious; we do not want to lose a minute of it.

5-Minute Activities!
A way to use every instructional minute

The following activities are flexible. They can be adjusted to different grade levels. Many can be either oral or written.

ALPHABET GAME

Let children take turns stating words in alphabetical order.

Apple, **B**all, **C**at, **D**og, **E**gg . . .

Vary this game by classifying words:

ANIMALS:
Alligator, **B**ear, **C**amel, **D**og, **E**lephant . . .

FRUITS:
Apple, **B**anana, **C**antaloupe . . .

FOOD:
Apple, **B**read, **C**ake . . .

I SPY

Play "I Spy" by asking students to find items in the room that . . .

- begin with the same letter
- are made of plastic
- are a certain shape
- are a particular color

I AM GOING ON A TRIP

The teacher begins by naming an item to take along that begins with "A." The students add to the list, one by one, in alphabetical order. To make this game harder for older students, ask them to REPEAT the previous items before adding their own.

TWENTY QUESTIONS

Think of a book title, school rule, or name of a song. Students try to identify it by asking up to twenty questions that can only be answered by *yes* or *no*.

SIMON SAYS

The teacher calls out a command. If the sentence begins with "Simon Says," the students follow the command. If it does not, the command is ignored.

Simon Says, "Stand on one foot!"
"Hop on the other!"

Try ending the game with "Simon Says, sit in your seats quietly."

LINING UP

Try lining up with a game:

> "If your favorite color is blue, please get in
> line."
> "Everyone wearing green, please line up."
> "All girls who are wearing ribbons, please line
> up."

You can use this as a follow-up to a skill you have
been teaching. If you have been working on
multiplication facts, each student could be given a
problem to answer (6 times 5) before lining up.

You may also dismiss students by having each
student state a playground rule, good health habit,
or a safety rule.

You can vary this by having each student name a
fruit, vegetable, flower, color, planet, country, state or
capital.

TICK - TACK - TOE

Write nine spelling words on the board. Have each
student draw a Tick-Tack-Toe grid and enter the
nine spelling words in any order. The teacher mixes
the words and then calls them out to the students.
The student that covers three words in a row wins.

MISSING VOWELS

Write words, phrases, titles of books on the board
without the vowels. Students decide which vowels
are missing.

T D Y S M N D Y

"C H R L T T ' S   W B"

SCRAMBLED WORDS

Have students scramble five of their spelling words, trade papers, and see how fast they can unscramble the words.

SYNONYMS AND ANTONYMS

Say a word. Call on a student to state its opposite word (antonym) or a word with a similar meaning (synonym).

MISSING NUMBERS

Say two numbers, such as 14 and 16.

Call on a student to fill in the missing number.

COUNTING

Have students either count in unison or individually by taking turns.

1

Count to 100.
Count backwards from 50 to 1.
Count to 100 by 10's, 5's, or 2's.

2

3

Vary this by saying the word "Oops!" on multiples of certain numbers:

Multiples of 5:
    1, 2, 3, 4, Oops!, 6, 7, 8, 9, Oops!, 11, 12, and so on.

RACING TO MAKE WORDS

Write a letter on the chalkboard. Students have two or three minutes to write as many words as they can that begin with that letter.

LISTEN CAREFULLY

Give three or more oral directions to the class and have the students follow your directions in unison.

Hop four times. Touch your left knee. Turn around twice.

FILL IN THE BLANKS

Display spelling words with missing letters on the chalkboard (a _ _ l e). Students complete as many words as they can within a time limit.

FINDING LITTLE WORDS IN BIG WORDS

Have students find as many little words as possible in the following by rearranging the letters:

Happy Birthday
Congratulations
Thanksgiving
Happy Holidays

Thanksgiving
1. an
2. sink
3. hang
4. has

FOLLOW THE SYMBOLS

This activity calls for coordinating visual directions with action.

X = Clap hands
O = Touch your head

1. XXXOX
2. XOXO
3. OOXO

DRAWING

Have students draw something made only of circles (or triangles, squares, rectangles).

CATEGORIES

Give the students three minutes to make a list of as many words as they can that are related to a general category such as *sports, animals, transportation, or seasons,* or to specific topics such as *football greats, animal habitats, winter fun, or favorite songs.*

ALL ABOUT ME

Have students print their first names vertically along the left margin of the paper. Then tell them to write a word or phrase that describes them that begins with each of the letters in their names.

Musical
Artistic
Rosy-complexioned
Youthful

WORD FAMILIES

See how many new words you can make from this base word in one minute:

_ _ a c k
(quack, black, stack)

Others: _ an, _ t, _ n, _ ent, _ ook, _ and

VOWELS

How many three-letter words can you think of using the vowel "A"?

_ a _
_ a _
_ a _

NAME GAME

Name something to eat (or wear or travel in) that begins with the first letter in your name.

Margie	milk
Joseph	jam
Charles	cheese

ENDING SOUNDS BEGIN NEW WORDS

The first student says a word that ends in a consonant.

The next student must say a word that BEGINS with the ending sound of the word just said.

BALL
LAP
PEN
NUT
TAP

Student Responses

In addition to five-minute activities, there are other ways to save valuable instruction time. Before teachers proceed to a new lesson or introduce a more difficult concept, they need to make sure that students clearly understand what has already been taught in the classroom. If teachers do not check for understanding, they will probably have to backtrack and reteach those students who were either confused or "lost," thus losing precious time.

Teachers often give written tests to determine how well students have mastered the skills taught. However, this usually calls for hours of grading papers weekly and scheduling classroom time to give students feedback and suggestions for improvement. Written tests are definitely needed periodically to show progress, but a simpler, more immediate method is necessary for use in daily lessons.

Response Cards

There are several ways to check for understanding while you are teaching. Many teachers make a set of response cards for each student in the classroom. These sets can be made from colored index cards with printed responses such as TRUE, FALSE, YES, NO, 1st, 2nd, 3rd, and so forth, inserted on large key rings or a chain. I like to use colored cards so I can see at a glance as I look around the classroom if everyone is holding up the TRUE (or PINK) index card.

There are many variations of this method. The age group with whom you are working is one factor that determines the strategy or materials you should use. For example, kindergarten and first grade students like to use cards with happy or sad faces when discussing feelings of characters in reading stories. They use cards with letters of the alphabet when working with beginning sounds.

The skill you are teaching will also dictate the types of response cards you will need. For example, when teaching about punctuating sentences in

Language Arts, you might want to use cards with a period, exclamation point, and a question mark. Then give a sentence and ask, "Which punctuation mark should go at the end of this sentence?"

Short, Written Answers

Miniature chalkboards and magic slates are excellent for students to respond with one or two word written answers. These objects seem to appeal to visual and kinesthetic learners, because students can see, hold, and manipulate them.

Almost all young people like to write with large magic markers. Place two or three markers plus some scrap paper in a 6" by 9" manila envelope for each student. Call out a question, and ask the students to write their answers on the paper. They should hold the answer chest high for you to see. My fifth and sixth grade students enjoyed writing the capitals of the states, contractions, division and multiplication facts in this way.

Hand Signals

Hand signals are responses that most students enjoy. "Thumbs-up, thumbs-down" is an old standby. Students hold their hands at chest level so no one else in the class can see their responses. If any student makes a mistake, he or she can correct it quickly to avoid embarrassment. The teacher says, "Put your thumbs up if you agree with this statement. Put your thumbs down if you do not."

Teachers get creative with their signals: "Wiggle your nose like a bunny if you agree with the answer." "Make a closed fist for *no* and an open palm for *yes*." "Open your eyes for *yes*; close them for *no*."

Immediate Feedback

When students respond to a question, the teacher scans the classroom to determine which children need additional help. The teacher then gives the correct response and discusses why this was the right answer.

Immediate feedback is important as it gives students the opportunity to correct any misconceptions they may have at the time. Students will not have to wait until test papers are graded, returned, and discussed in order to find out the skills in which they need help.

Remember that these methods of group responses involving one or two word answers or signals should never take the place of the students responding to questions using higher order thinking skills. These strategies are only employed to determine if students understand the lesson content up to that point. When the teacher is assured that the majority of the class comprehends the lesson being presented, the students will be asked to analyze, evaluate, and apply their new knowledge, as usual.

I find that good classroom teachers vary their students' response strategies periodically to hold interest and keep motivation high. The clock is ticking, and time is precious. Lost time cannot be reclaimed. Our children deserve every minute that we can give them. If you agree with this last paragraph, "Wiggle your nose!"

My Favorite Teacher

My Recipe For Teachers . . .
(from memory)
by
Roger McCandless

When asked about favorite teachers, two individuals immediately spring to mind: Walter Pray and Mr. Martin. Never were two teachers so different, physically, socially, and pedagogically.

Walt Pray was a high school speech teacher. He was handsome (all the high school girls had crushes . . .), eloquent, and refined. Walt Pray was a perfect role model for his students. I never heard him embarrass a student. His criticism and praise were totally constructive. He focused on the work, not the student. I think this was perhaps the most important lesson I ever learned about teaching.

Mr. Martin (I don't know if any student ever knew his first name!) was in many ways the antithesis of Walter Pray. He was a stern, forbidding hulk of a science teacher who also coached junior varsity football. Square-jawed, with piercing eyes, Mr. Martin was very effective in a different way. He had the complete respect and attention of his students. It was his custom to have oral spot-checks on the previous night's reading assignment. He would call on us randomly and ask one question. Your day's grade depended upon your answer. For the unprepared, this was a terrifying time, because the flash of disapproval from those penetrating eyes was perhaps more devastating than the zero he put into the register. After all, we never actually saw the zero.

What I learned from Mr. Martin was the value of expectancy. We were expected to have our lessons . . . no excuses . . . so, by and large, we had them. And from Walt Pray, I learned to focus on the work or the problem, not on the individual.

I carried what I learned from these two teachers into my own teaching. Two teachers, two completely different styles, yet both very effective and memorable.

Part IX

TAKING A
BREAK

*Even Teachers
Need a Recess!*

Life Isn't Always
A Bowl Of Cherries

Teaching, with all of its positive and satisfying qualities, can be a stressful profession. There are endless demands on teachers, coupled with daily crises. These conditions, added to crowded classrooms and inadequate supplies, can very well produce frustrated, tired, and stressed-out teachers.

Periodically, I see articles in magazines and newspapers on the most stressful jobs in America. On several occasions, the inner-city school teachers were rated number one in regard to their level of stress. Although inner-city teachers were targeted, I believe that no teachers are immune.

Many times a teacher can identify the specific reasons for stress. Problems can be alleviated or conditions can be changed that will reduce the level of stress. There are, however, some situations that we cannot control or change, at least not immediately. Let's look at some examples. If a teacher is working in a school and having a personality conflict with the principal, the teacher may not be able to improve the relationship or transfer to another school to avoid this situation. If a teacher is assigned to a grade level or subject that is not satisfactory to the teacher, a request for a reassignment may not be possible until the end of the school year. Or if a teacher is burdened with too many professional duties or personal problems, it may take time to reduce or solve them.

It would be futile to go into the "whys" of stress, for there are probably as many reasons as there are individual cases. From too many personal obligations to too little job respect, the reasons are endless.

Therefore, we may be better served here to explore ways that teachers can manage and cope with stressful situations in their daily lives. On the following pages we will examine some of these methods.

Ways To Manage Stress

Look on the Sunny Side.

Try to be positive in the way you relate and respond to others. Don't clutter up your mind with negative thoughts. Being critical of others and harboring negative opinions can become a habit that is difficult to change.

Personally, I believe that it is healthier to be around positive people. I gravitate to individuals who are happy with themselves and appreciative of others and their achievements. I am more comfortable with people who see the half-full, rather than the half-empty glass. I like people who build, rather than tear down. Please protect me from the moaning, groaning, naysaying, doomsday people who delight in finding fault with everyone and everything.

I believe that if individuals strive to develop strong, positive personalities, they will be better equipped to deal with anything that comes their way. They will face problems in the same manner that they face the world—with a healthy attitude and a positive outlook. By learning to look on the sunny side, individuals can help counteract the negative effects of stress.

Give Yourself an Attaboy!

Validate your own actions. Don't depend on others to give you approval for your behavior. Look within yourself for this. Let's look at the following scenario and see how this applies:

> You volunteer to chair the fifth grade
> Clothesline Art Show. You work for
> weeks, staying after school many
> afternoons. You really want everything
> to be perfect. On the day of the art
> show, your principal is out of town and
> does not see the results of all your hard
> work. You are disappointed, angry, and
> later, depressed. You feel that if the
> principal had been there, he would
> have praised your efforts.

Ask yourself why you volunteered for this project. What was your motive? Were your efforts for the kids or to gain praise from your principal and peers? Perhaps it was for both.

Granted, we all need praise from time to time. But life doesn't always give us an audience for each of our successes. When we mow the lawn, the neighbors on our block don't stop what they are doing to cheer for us. When we clean the house, very few of us get three curtain calls and a bouquet of roses. And when we have that perfect lesson when everything just clicks, there is usually no fellow teacher, supervisor, or principal there to see it and applaud.

Oftentimes, we must look within ourselves for this applause. We must learn to boost our own egos. Sometimes we must just look in the mirror and give ourselves an "attaboy!" for our efforts. Or do as one sixth grade teacher told his class: "Take your right hand and put it on your left shoulder. Now pat yourself on the back for a job well done!"

Don't Bite Off More Than You Can Chew!

Learn to say "No!" It is easy to overextend yourself and become involved in too many projects or activities. It's often difficult to say no, especially to a principal or supervisor, but sometimes you must if you are to keep your life in balance.

A friend of mine told me how she handled a situation with her principal when he asked her to chair another committee. The following was her "softer way" of saying no:

> "I won't be available to chair the Spring
> Carnival Committee this year. If you
> remember, I am already assigned to—
> and very much involved with—two
> other school committees so I would not

be able to devote the time necessary to chairing the project. However, I plan to attend the carnival, and I'll be happy to do my share by manning one of the booths that day."

In the above case, the teacher said "no" to another committee assignment, but softened her statement by offering to help in a role that involved no preparation.

We are all expected to do our share to make our schools run smoothly, but all too often good workers, because they are such good workers, end up doing more than their share. By dividing up the work and giving everyone an "opportunity to serve," we will have fewer teachers who are overworked and pressured.

Learn to be an "Escape Artist."

Once in a while, you just need to get away from the problem or problems that are causing you stress. Yes, they will still be there when you return, but a brief respite from them might help you view them in a clearer light.

Try to build in some breaks in your daily schedule. Designate a few minutes here and a few minutes there as *YOUR* time. Use this time to do something nice for yourself! An exercise class, a hot bath, a nap, a stroll through the mall, a trip to your favorite book store, a dinner out, a golf game - any of these activities will give you a change of pace and return you to your world with a healthier outlook and renewed energy and enthusiasm.

One of your "breaks" should be between school and home. It is difficult to work all day, attend a faculty meeting, fight traffic, and arrive home to face cleaning the house or cooking supper. Too many people jump from one situation to another with no beneficial transition time. Try to take a few minutes to acclimate yourself to another environment. Set aside a few minutes between jobs to feed the birds, sit in a swing and talk to your children about their day, or just *enjoy the moment.* Remember, even teachers need a recess!

Establish Some Meaningful Long-term Goals.

Many of us are spending the majority of our time on trivial, but necessary, activities. Take time to write down everything you do for just *one day*, and you will agree that this is true.

Look at the following partial list of duties. These activities are necessary to the daily life of this individual, but they are not helping to achieve some greater purpose in life:

Wrapped a birthday present
Picked up some groceries at the store
Called Time of Day to set the clock
Watched the news on TV
Took out the trash
Paid telephone bill

Cleaned out a drawer
Wrote a thank you note to a friend
Prepared a casserole for dinner

Sometimes we are stressed because we do not believe we are accomplishing anything of importance. We know that we are always busy, but we don't feel that we are getting anywhere. We realize that these activities are necessary, but sometimes they take all of our time, leaving little time for things of value. If our lives become inundated with trivial activities, we begin to feel that we are not in control, and eventually, we get frustrated and depressed.

Life must have meaningful direction. If we have long-term goals, we give it purpose. Think of some things that you want to accomplish during your lifetime, and write these down. Let's look at a list of personal goals written by a middle-school teacher from North Carolina:

I want to get my Master's Degree.

I want to gain expertise in using a computer.

I want to build a deck on my house so I can entertain easier in the summer.

I want to become healthier and more physically fit.

These are large goals but they can be broken down into smaller segments that can be easily accomplished. To achieve the goal of becoming healthier, this teacher could begin an exercise program, alter his diet to include more fruits and vegetables, or learn how to balance his active life with rest and relaxation. If he walked the track a few times a week, he would be working toward one of his long-term goals in life. And what a feeling of accomplishment he would have!

There are many small, insignificant activities that disrupt and intrude on our lives. Many are necessary, but they should not be all-consuming. We must set our priorities and schedule our time so we can do the important things in life in addition to everyday duties. Therefore, it is essential that individuals set clear goals with specific ways to achieve them in order to take control and have a more satisfying and meaningful life.

Hang in There.

Sometimes we get so wrapped up in our problems that we lose our perspective. We usually need to take a step backwards and look at the problem in relation to everything else. We want to remember that although things may be bad at the time, nothing lasts forever. Time heals; and situations change. What was a terrible problem on Monday may be history by Friday.

Therefore, we may need to bide our time and wait until a situation plays itself out. This is where coping skills are so effective. Let's look at a situation that occurs fairly often in various school systems and review the ways we can respond to it.

Susan Bell has just been hired as a first year teacher and assigned to an elementary school near her apartment. She is very excited about her new job. The week before school starts, she spends every afternoon and all day Saturday fixing up her classroom.

School begins. Susan loves her fourth grade students. She likes her principal and fellow teachers. Everything is going great!

On the fifth day of school, Susan hears a rumor that enrollment is down, and there is a good possibility that a teacher may be transferred to another school. Susan is devastated. She remembers the old saying, "last hired, first fired!"

When she goes home that afternoon, Susan is both angry and depressed—angry that she could be the one that has to pack up and leave after all the work that she did on her classroom and depressed because she feels that she doesn't have any control over events.

After a few moments of self pity, Susan decides to get hold of herself. She reminds herself that this is only a rumor and may not be true. She tells herself that although she may not have control over the events themselves, she does have control over *how she responds* to them.

Susan sits down and makes a list of the ways she will handle this problem during the next few days if, in fact, it does materialize. These are her coping skills for dealing with a stressful situation.

Susan's Survival Skills

Be Positive. Don't dwell on the negative. After all, this may not even happen to me. Some other teacher may decide he or she desires a transfer to be closer to home.

Don't let rumors upset me, and continue to do the good job I am doing now. Until I find out, I will give 100 percent to my kids, my lessons, and my present school.

Don't take any of this personally. It's so easy to think a person is transferred because of something he did or did not do. I will remember that this is a common occurrence resulting from a decrease in the number of students the school expects to enroll.

Don't assign blame to anyone. It's no one's fault. Never say anything that will be regretted later. Remember, you can't unring the bell!

Keep busy! Exercise! Think good thoughts!

If I do get "chosen," I'll take it in stride. I will remember what I have always believed: *when one door closes, another opens*. I love my present school, but maybe the new school will be even better.

And Finally, Realize that Laughter Really is the Best Medicine.

For all of life's ups and downs, laughter is the great leveler. The most well-balanced, uncomplicated, unaffected people I have ever known were the wonderful individuals who knew how to laugh. I like these people, for they are open, candid, active participants in life. They know that life is too short to waste time worrying or fretting. They look for the humor in situations. And believe me, there is *always* humor.

The following articles are included for your enjoyment. They show that life should not be taken so seriously, and it's okay to laugh at yourself and with others. The last story is one of my favorites. It sends the message that during life's highs and lows and successes and failures, all we are really expected to do is to keep a positive attitude and "do the best we can!"

Let's All Sit Up Straight

After twenty-five years of working in elementary schools, I find that my vocabulary has become extremely limited. I depend on words such as come, go, stop it, no!, use your tissue, raise your hands, and can't you hold it?

I feel comfortable with sit down, lower your voice, open your books, turn to page —, clear your desks, turn around, don't call out your answers, and I said *no!* I rely on directives such as line up, time out, drink your milk, let's get a little quiet, close your books, and *I mean NO!*

Edward Dolch, author and educator, listed 220 words that he believed primary children should master. I'm afraid that my vocabulary has dwindled down to a number that is now less than my waist size.

I am also depending more and more on *teacher phrases*. These are not too noticeable in a school setting, but they are rather obvious in a social situation.

Let's look at some examples of my recent behavior . . .

At a sale in a department store

"Don't *even* think about pushing or shoving. If you do, you will have to go to the back of the line."

At a restaurant

"I hope you remembered to wash your hands. Now use your napkin like a good boy, and let me cut up your meat for you."

In a doctor's waiting room during the flu season

"Everyone take a tissue and cover your face when you sneeze; and sir, please don't *ever* let me see you wipe your nose on your sleeve again!"

At a social gathering

"Let's use our best auditorium manners and talk quietly to our neighbors."

At church

"Now let's all sit up straight and give the nice man our undivided attention."

At a party

"Please, don't swish your olive around; you know it's not nice to play with your food."

At a business meeting

"Clear your desks, lay your pencils down, and let's all put on our *thinking caps.*"

When leaving a movie theater

"I like the way Marsha and Bertie are placing their popcorn boxes and candy wrappers in the big trash containers on each side of the aisle."

Giving directions to a lost motorist

"I will give you these directions once and *only* once. I will *not* repeat them. You must listen the *first* time. Are you ready? Now, turn left at the corner and . . ."

At a riot

"None of this would have happened if you had remembered Rule #1: '*Always keep your hands and feet to yourself!*'"

I Want to Come Back As a Peabody Duck

I had my first glimpse of the "Peabody Ducks" while attending the International Reading Association National Convention in Orlando, Florida, in 1992. The ducks have been a tradition at the Peabody Hotels in Orlando and Memphis, Tennessee, for over fifty years.

They swim and splash around in the fountain in the lobby of the hotel all day. At five o'clock in the afternoon, the red carpet is rolled out for them, and the ducks parade to a marching tune back to the elevator that takes them up to their rooms at the top of the hotel. What a life! This poem was written in the lobby of the Peabody Hotel:

I Want to Come Back
As a Peabody Duck

The Peabody Ducks
   Are a sight to behold!
No cares and no worries,
   And worth more than gold.

They preen and they primp;
   They shimmy and shake.
They're spoiled little darlings,
   Just make no mistake.

No lessons to plan,
   No papers to grade,
Just pose for the cameras,
   And twice daily parade.

In the finest hotel,
   They reside and are fed.
In return, they duck-walk
   Down a carpet of red.

No tears to wipe,
   No noses that run . . .
Just splash in the fountain
   And play and have fun.

Oh Lord, here's my prayer,
   And with a little luck,
Let me come back some day
   As a Peabody Duck.

Do The Best You Can

I had always heard that we, as educators, receive much more than we give, learn much more than we teach. I accepted this as a truism. The words always seemed to give a nice, positive ending to speeches given by educators to other educators at conference banquets in convention halls. In other words, I really never gave much thought to the real meaning of these words.

Until this year. Until Sandy.

Sandy is a rather large, six-year-old kindergarten child. He is in perpetual motion. He is always laughing and giggling. Life is a joy to Sandy. He is the original "Happy Face!"

Every morning at eleven o'clock, I can hear Sandy bouncing down the halls, chanting, "Do the best you can! Do the best you can!" The chant gets louder and louder until he enters the office and jumps at the school secretary and me, yelling "Boo!" Then he bursts into laughter as we pretend to be surprised. He comes to the office to get his daily medicine for hyperactivity.

We chat with him for awhile and he leaves, skipping and singing, "Do the best you can!"

I asked his kindergarten teacher where the chant originated. She said that many times Sandy couldn't do as well as the other children so she told him not to worry but to do the best he could. The words stuck and apparently Sandy lives by them.

Sandy will be leaving us at the end of the year. He and his mother are moving. I will miss him. I will always remember that when he was around me, I felt good. I laughed.

I liked the way I could always set my clock by him. I knew it was eleven o'clock when I heard that singsong chant coming down the hall.

I liked his predictability. I liked his happy face. I liked the way he lit up our office, even on a dark, rainy, hectic Monday morning.

I have learned a lot from this positive little bundle of energy. In this complicated, high-tech, stressful, competitive society, this uncomplicated little boy was saying not to worry . . . just do the best you can . . . *do the best you can.*

My Favorite Teacher

Miss Katie
by
Mary Carnes

I'll always remember Miss Katie. She was my first grade teacher in 1916. She was beautiful with blond hair piled high on her head and held in place by a jeweled comb. She wore such pretty clothes and smelled like spring flowers.

She was always smiling and happy. On pretty days we would all eat our lunch on the school grounds, and Miss Katie sat in the circle with us. She would tell us stories about when she was a little girl. As we listened to her, we would move closer and closer until we were almost sitting on her lap.

Miss Katie liked to cook. She asked each of us to bring our Mama's favorite recipes for cookies, and she promised to make us some. I took three recipes for cookies and one for taffy kisses. Later Miss Katie did bring the class some cookies, but I think she bought them.

Miss Katie chose me to be a "sweet pea" for our end-of-the-year play. I was so excited because I got to wear a pink crepe-paper hat and bob my head up and down like a flower dancing in the wind. I can remember that play even today. Miss Katie was so special to me.

Part X

LOOKING
AHEAD

*Preparing
for a New Era*

A Look to the Future

As we begin the 21st Century, we are astounded by the social, economic, and political changes taking place globally, particularly in the areas of technology and communication. These changes will definitely affect the future roles of teachers and schools.

Let's consider the great strides being made in the areas of technology and communication. We need only to look around us to see that we are living in an era where pagers, electronic mail, and cellular phones are accepted components of modern life. In this age of information, technology is increasingly changing the way we live, work, and learn.

The Role of the Teacher

How will technology affect the way we educate our students? We can no longer think of schools as they were in the past. We are living in an era of new challenges, opportunities, and problems. Individuals must have the necessary skills and knowledge to survive, grow, and prosper, and our educational system must meet these needs.

The teacher's role will expand. It will include having a greater understanding of technology and how to integrate it in the classroom. It will involve having a more active participation in curriculum development, a voice in policy making and administrative decisions, and a practical understanding of conflict resolution and improving relationships among people.

Incorporating Technology in the Classroom

Teachers in the 21st Century will no longer have a choice of whether to become computer literate, for the computer has become essential to learning.

Advances in computer and communication technologies will continue to influence the structure and content of our classrooms.

We will see an increased use of multimedia and integrated technologies in the classroom. We are moving toward transportable equipment and a wireless society where it will be possible for our students to access worldwide information, whenever and wherever they choose.

What is important today is not how many computers a classroom has but how they are being used to help children learn and prepare for the real world. Studies of classrooms that are effectively using computers are resulting in positive research data. For example, a ten-year research project by Apple Computer, Inc., released in 1995, showed that students with access to computers and other high-tech tools learn faster, test better, and are absent less. This was the longest ongoing project of its kind. Researchers at 25 universities studied a dozen kindergarten through 12th grade classes during this time period. The project reported that the use of computer technology fostered student collaboration and resulted in classrooms that were more active learning environments.

Although these are good things to hear, we must be cautious in our rush to computerize classrooms. Young people today are comfortable in the digital age; however, many of our teachers are not. Before we dump computers into the classroom, we must *first* train teachers so they will become confident, not only in the mechanics of operating the machines, but in their knowledge of how technology can bring subjects to life and stimulate the process of learning and discovery.

The training of teachers should result in their making wise choices in how to use technology in classrooms. The computer is an engaging and effective tool, but a critical role of the teacher is to make sure computers fit our educational needs, rather than trying to fit our needs to the machines. To accomplish this, clear goals concerning what we expect from technology in education must be established.

One of the goals of education should be to elevate students from the simpler levels of learning, such as knowledge and comprehension, to higher levels of thinking. Technology can be used to free students from mundane tasks and give them more time to focus on these higher levels. When individuals don't have to spend inordinate amounts of time locating information, they will have more time to organize and evaluate it. We all have observed students in the library spending hours and hours gathering information, then hurrying to put it together in some acceptable form to meet a class deadline. With the changes in accessing information, we can shift our emphasis from locating data to the higher-level mental processes of assimilation, organization, correlation, and evaluation.

To reach the goal of enhancing the learning process through the use of technology, teachers must be given adequate time to study the best ways to integrate technology in the classroom and develop new ways to teach and assess students' progress. Only through comprehensive staff development programs can we prepare teachers for the changes that will accompany the widespread use of technology.

Assuming an Active Role in Curriculum Development

In the years ahead, we will see overwhelming changes taking place in the world. To make sure that our curriculum reflects these changes, the 21st Century teacher must have an active role in curriculum development.

The time has passed when we asked students to memorize facts. We are living in a world of instant communication where countries, governments, leaders, and ideologies change from day to day. Facts change rapidly and may, within days, not be facts anymore. The time has come for studying the big picture - for investigating, understanding, and evaluating the *hows* and *whys* of the world.

The focus of teaching is changing from disseminating knowledge to helping students *learn how to learn* so education will be a continuous, lifelong process. Teachers will help students develop skills for thinking, reasoning, solving problems, making appropriate decisions, analyzing and evaluating data. Our students must be able to research problems, work cooperatively, and communicate effectively. The role of the teacher in the future will change from instructor to facilitator as students are empowered to assume more and more responsibility for their own learning.

Having a Greater Voice in Policy-Making and Administrative Practices

The 21st Century teacher will have a greater voice in policy-making and in the way schools are administered. Instead of a centrally managed school system, the structure of schools will lean more toward school-based management, shared decision-making, on-site management, or whatever term is used to describe management styles where decisions are made by the people most directly affected by them. Flexibility is one of the best features of this management structure. Therefore, it can take a variety of forms according to the problems to be addressed and what is best for the specific communities.

Local control is necessary so parents and teachers can be more involved in scheduling, curricular, and budgeting decisions. It would be possible for decentralization to be carried out to the degree that the school sites became autonomous. The central administration offices could be converted into service centers where books, equipment, media, supervisory assistance, and other resources could be requisitioned by the individual schools to enhance instruction.

We've known for a long time that top-down mandates are not effective. They do not take into account the necessity for changing attitudes, behaviors, or values. It's only common sense to give the individuals who are expected to implement the programs a voice in the decisions.

Let's look at one example of a top-down mandate that hit a few snags in some schools a few years back. In the 1960s, there was an outpouring of federal funds which supported innovative and experimental educational programs. Among these were the Right to Read Program, Head Start, and Follow Through. During this time, also, there was the growth of alternative schools which broke away from the practices of conventional or traditional schools and approached teaching and learning in a different way.

One of these alternative approaches was a move toward nongraded classrooms, team teaching, and open space buildings. These schools were organized along the philosophy of informal or open education.

The physical layout of conventional classrooms seemed to hinder open classrooms. Walls were thought to be physical barriers. Space was needed to allow teachers to share children and equipment and to allow students to flow back and forth between the classroom areas. Many new schools were constructed that used space in freer and more flexible ways. In older schools, the traditional walls were removed, leaving more usable space for teachers and children.

A group of administrators in Tennessee went on a fact-finding trip to learn more about these schools. They toured several regions in the United States where open education schools were located and supposedly thriving. To the administrators' surprise, they found that the teachers in some of these schools had, over time, built the walls back between the learning areas. They divided these areas with stacks of books, media kits, book cases, chart holders, and even cardboard boxes.

Several administrators in the group asked the teachers why they were partitioning off the rooms. The administrators found that when the decision came down to try this instructional change, the teachers in these schools had not been asked to participate in the initial planning and preparation stages or to assist in any of the decision-making processes. In addition, they had never been given the time or training to commit to this new way of teaching that they were being asked to implement. By rebuilding the walls, the teachers were having the last word!

Teachers, therefore, *must* have a voice in their own destiny. Who knows and understands best the needs of a school than the people who work there?

The individuals who are in daily, constant contact with the students and parents in a school setting - the custodians, cafeteria workers, support staff members, teachers, and principals - are the most knowledgeable of the *real issues* that drive the school.

Resolving Conflicts and Helping to Improve Relationships Among People

As our nation grows older, its population increases and diversifies. These demographic changes often introduce new challenges to our lives. People must learn to live optimally with individuals of other races, nationalities, and cultures.

The teacher of the 21st Century must have the skills necessary to deal with relationships and conflicts among individuals. Today's young people face many problems, many of which were unheard of fifty years ago. At that time, discipline problems in our schools centered around students chewing gum, forgetting to raise hands to speak, running in the halls, and occasional arguments or fist fights. These problems seem trivial now that we are dealing with teen pregnancy, suicide, rape, dropouts, gangs, drugs, alcohol abuse, racial tensions, and school violence.

Violence in America and in our schools is a legitimate concern, especially since the *severity* of incidents seems to be escalating, and young people are displaying inappropriate behavior at an earlier age. We hear reports almost daily about students bringing guns into schools and about kids killing kids. When these tragedies occur, the community is horrified. Students are traumatized. Teachers become disillusioned and disheartened and often quit in despair.

These tragedies must not be allowed to occur. Schools must do what they have to do to restore order. Safety must be the number one priority. If this means installing metal detectors at every school entrance and policemen on every floor in order to remove offenders, then we must do so if this will return out-of-control schools to normalcy. But these are only interim measures, not solutions to long-term problems. In the meantime, we need to dig deeper, root out the causes, and take measures to permanently correct them. Our students *must* be safe from harm, for no one can learn in a climate of intimidation, fear, or terror.

Perhaps we need to take a closer look at the size of schools. Bigger is not always better. Too often, students get lost in the maze of large schools. They begin to feel isolated, lonely, and useless. They drop out or become discipline problems. And yet we continue to close small schools under the guise of cost efficiency. What does it matter how financially sound a school appears on paper if we have dissolved the glue that held the organization together?

The environment of small schools supports the acts of teaching and learning. Smaller classes and smaller schools result in stronger personal relationships between teachers and students, less discipline problems, and a more manageable learning community. In the small schools I visited, the staff and students believed that they were part of a close-knit school family.

However, even in the best of circumstances, many of our young people have greater responsibilities and pressures on them than we realize. We know of children acting as substitute parents for other siblings and of teenagers trying to balance almost full-time after-school jobs with family and school responsibilities. In many cases, children are being forced to grow up too fast. They are bombarded with a tremendous number of decisions to make. Sometimes a wrong choice can adversely affect a child's entire future.

There are no easy answers to the problems young people face, for the problems are often complicated and far-reaching. Teachers need to be highly trained in conflict resolution and counseling skills. They may need additional training about how students' behavior is affected by their background, family structure, culture, needs, and values. Mentor teachers need to be assigned to small groups of students to give them someone they can turn to for advice or individual assistance when they have problems or concerns. All teachers must learn to *listen* to students.

In the American public education system, we educate *all* the children. It is an American tradition that has made our nation great. In accepting all children, we accept all their problems. These problems often accompany children to school, resulting in an increase of discipline incidents and a lowering of school morale.

Each child deserves our best. We must do all in our power to revitalize our schools and create an environment that is a safe haven for children where education is highly valued and cherished by all.

The Good Stories

It worries me that we seldom hear about the good things that are happening in our schools across the nation. The child with the gun makes the front page of the newspaper; the school vandalized by students is the leading television story for three days.

These are the sensational stories, the headliners, but they aren't the big stories. The important ones are the stories I was privileged to witness as I traveled from school to school and talked to teachers, principals, custodians, secretaries, staff members, parents, and students. They are the stories of individuals who display love, respect, warmth, and understanding for children on a *daily* basis. And they are the stories of children—yours, mine, ours—who look to teachers and other school people for that support, leadership, encouragement, and inspiration.

These are the stories that we seldom hear but are crying out to be heard. I have tried to tell some of them in this book. And there are other good things happening right now in big schools, little schools, rich and poor ones, rural and urban ones, all across this land.   These are the stories of love, courage, and strength that reinforce my faith in the American educational system.

A New Era

As we begin our journey in this millennium—this exciting and complex time—each day will offer us opportunities to become involved in the challenges and changes of our society. We will see changes in education—changes in programs, policies, and technology. Some changes will be good; others will not. New methods and strategies will surface, while others will vanish.

Change, change, change. Life is about evolving, growing, and moving on to the next place. As we gain new knowledge and learn new ways of doing and thinking about things, the cycle of change continues.

Amidst this change, the only constant on which we can depend is the teacher. For even in a world of technology, our children need the human factor for interaction and personal communication that only the teacher can provide. Therefore, the teacher must remain the stable force in this era.

It will be the teacher's role, no matter what form it might take in the 21st Century, to guide, advise, counsel, instruct, nudge, cajole, dare, lead, push, encourage, and inspire individuals to be the best that they can be.

"All eyes up here, please.
We are ready to begin."

RESOURCES

Literary and Human Resources

Literary Resources:

A good professional library is essential to anyone in education. I examined my library and selected a sampling of books that are interesting and inspirational to read. The books and articles marked with an asterisk (*) were used as references in *All Eyes Up Here!* However, all of the books listed helped shape my philosophy for teaching.

If you are beginning your library, it is my personal opinion that you might enjoy having these books as a foundation on which to build your own collection.

Brookover, Wilbur; Beamer, Laurence; Efthin, Helen; Hathaway, Douglas; Lezotte, Lawrence; Miller, Stephen; Passalacqua, Joseph; and Louis Tornatzky. *Creating Effective Schools.* Holmes Beach, FL: Learning Publications, Inc., 1982.

Canfield, Jack and Mark Victor Hansen. *Chicken Soup for the Soul.* Deerfield Beach, FL: Health Communications, Inc., 1993.

Canfield, Jack and Harold C. Wells. *101 Ways to Enhance Self-Concept in the Classroom: A Handbook for Teachers and Parents.* Englewood Cliffs, NJ: Prentice-Hall, Inc., 1976.

Conari Press-Editors. *Random Acts of Kindness.* Berkeley, CA: Conari Press, 1993.

Conroy, Pat. *The Water is Wide.* Boston: Houghton Mifflin, 1972.

Covey, Stephen R. *The 7 Habits of Highly Effective People: Restoring the Character Ethic.* New York: Simon & Shuster, Fireside Edition, 1989.

Deal, Terrence E. and Allen A. Kennedy, *Corporate Cultures: The Rites and Rituals of Corporate Life.* Reading, MA: Addison-Wesley, 1982.

Fulghum, Robert. *All I Really Need to Know I Learned in Kindergarten.* New York: Ivy Books, 1986.

Ginott, Dr. Haim G. *Teacher & Child.* New York: Collier Books (Quality Paperbacks, 1993), 1973. *

"In Celebration of Education," The Lancaster News Special Edition. May 22, 1992. *

Lightfoot, Sara Lawrence. *The Good High School: Portraits of Character and Culture.* New York: Basic Books, 1983.

Lortie, Dan. *Schoolteacher.* Chicago: University of Chicago Press, 1975.

McPhee, John. *The Headmaster.* New York: Farrar, Strauss & Giroux, 1966.

Medley, H. Anthony. *Sweaty Palms: The Neglected Art of Being Interviewed.* Belmont, CA: Lifetime Learning Publications (Division of Wadsworth Publishing Company, Inc.), 1978. *

Miller, Leslie. "Higher Learning," USA TODAY. September 14, 1995. *

Murphy, Elspeth Campbell. *Chalkdust.* Grand Rapids, MI: Baker Book House, 1979.

Murphy, Elspeth Campbell. *Recess.* Grand Rapids, MI: Baker Book House, 1988.

Nelsen, Jane. *Positive Discipline.* New York: Ballantine Books, 1981.

Peck, M. Scott. *The Road Less Traveled.* New York: Simon & Shuster, 1978.

Peters, Tom and Nancy Austin. *A Passion for Excellence: The Leadership Difference.* New York: Random House, 1985. *

Peters, Thomas J. and Robert H. Waterman, Jr. *In Search of Excellence: Lessons From America's Best Run Companies.* New York: Harper Collins Publishers (Warner Books edition), 1982. *

Routman, Regie. *Invitations: Changing as Teachers and Learners.* Portsmouth, NH: Heinemann Educational Books, Inc., 1994.

Routman, Regie. *Transitions.* Portsmouth, NH: Heinemann Educational Books, Inc., 1988.

Trelease, Jim. *The New Read-Aloud Handbook.* New York: Penguin Books, 1989.

Wong, Harry K. and Rosemary Tripi Wong. *The First Days of School: How to be an Effective Teacher.* Sunnyvale, CA: Harry K. Wong Publications, 1991.

Human Resources:

Human resources are the most valuable of all, because only people can give us the benefit of their experiences, feelings, beliefs, views, values, and passions. The following individuals were instrumental in this book:

Jack Carr

The members of my family—the Carr, Myers, Carnes, Smithson, and Vlasis clans

The faculty and staff of Saint Elmo Elementary School

The faculty and staff of Chattanooga Elementary School

The wonderful student teachers I was fortunate to supervise at The University of Tennessee at Chattanooga

The supervising teachers who, through their partnerships with student teachers, gave their time, attention, encouragement, and creative ideas both to them and to me

The dedicated teachers and principals from the numerous schools I visited in Tennessee, Georgia, North Carolina, and South Carolina

I wish I could mention all of you by name, but the list of educators would be longer than this book. However, I want to express my gratitude to each of you for taking time to share your classroom strategies, instructional methods, and hopes for the future.

A special thanks goes to Sherry Hulgan for her delightful illustrations of children and teachers.

My deepest appreciation is extended to Marsha Brumlow for her expertise, technical skills, and invaluable suggestions for improvement.

The following individuals were crucial for their technical and editorial assistance:

Beth Smithson and Charlotte Vlasis
Gene Beatey, Bertie Floyd, and Linda Burton
Fred Carr, Richard Carnes, and Allen Carr
Mary Carnes, Paula and Pete Carnes

The following teachers, principals, and staff members gave me specific ideas over the years from their classrooms and schools for excellent teaching and leadership strategies:

Martha Dyer Kaiser, Amanda Cate, Sharon Vaughn, Lou Perfetti, Dr. Kathleen Conner, Pamelia Howard, Judy Sivils, Peggy Anderson, Carolyn Carroll, Gloria Morris, Sylvia Kubic, Linda Montieth, Mary Ann Graham, Rose Marie Coleman, Bill Hodges, Eunice Hodges, Deborah Horton, Dan Waggoner, Opal Shaw, Brenda Kaye, Cecile Flanders, Kathy Dums, Leslie Murphy, Missy Jones, Donna Trick, Faye Weaver Brown, Naomi Hay, Sammy Gooden, Linda Hardison, Linda Hawkes, Rebecca Everett, Dr. Jack Conner, Lonita Davidson, Luther Shockley, Joyce Lancaster, Mary Jo Green, Pemmy Patten, Lu Lewis, Jessie Hearn, Beverly Smith, Bob Hope, Anna Carothers,

Joe Bean, Janet Tindell, Eleanor Barnes, Anna Ritchie, Aaron Washington, Janie Holder and daughter, Kim, Ernest Mathis, Jr., Mickey Haddock, Tommy Wolfe, Papa De Shazo, Jackie Palmer, Hardin Satterfield, Mary Uchytil, Angelo Napolitano, Caroline Ellis, Julia Olive, Jeanne Dixon, and Jane Loudermilk

These wonderful individuals shared the stories of their favorite teachers with us:

Dr. C. C. Bond, Marcia Kling, Dalton Roberts, Julius Parker, Roger McCandless, Linda Knowles, Mary Carnes, and Dr. Clifford Hendrix, Jr.

I saved the best until last, for the most valuable individuals of all are the *children*. We look to them, we learn from them, and we plan for them. They are our reasons for being in the profession of education.

We must never lose sight of the fact that as teachers, principals, school boards, superintendents, or parents, we must always focus on *what is best for our children* if we are to be successful as a school system, a community, or as a nation.

INDEX

Permissions   *(continued from page ii)*

Excerpt from article entitled *"Is Kindness Out of Style?"* by Julius Parker in the <u>Chattanooga Free Press</u> on September 24, 1995. Reprinted by permission of Julius Parker.

"The Teacher Who Changed My Life" by Dalton Roberts from his book *Things That Really Matter.* © 1986. Reprinted by permission of Dalton Roberts.

Reference to management style in *A Passion For Excellence* by Thomas Peters and Nancy Austin (1985). Reprinted by permission of Random House.

Permission for use of BAND-AID®, registered trademark, granted from Johnson & Johnson.

Children's names were changed to protect them from fame.

Another book about teachers and kids that will touch your heart and your funnybone. A must-read for everyone who loves and cares about children.

How Come The Wise Men Are In The DEMPSTER DUMPSTER®?
by
Dr. Tee Carr

Yes, there *really* was a school with great teachers and neat kids where laughter, love, and learning reigned supreme. And there *really* was a cat who charmed a sixth grade class of ring-tailed-tooters into becoming a model of exemplary behavior. And there *really* were three Wise Men in the DEMPSTER DUMPSTER®.

Tee says these are all undeniable *facts*. Anyway, that's her story and she's sticking to it!

To purchase, use order form on the following page.

Book Order Form

There's nothing like having your own personal copy of Tee Carr's *All Eyes Up Here!* Then you can make notes in it and refer to it whenever the need arises. If you want additional copies for yourself or as a gift for someone, complete the form below and send it with your check or money order to CARR Enterprises.

You'll also want to have a copy of Tee's wonderful book, *How Come the Wise Men Are In The DEMPSTER DUMPSTER®?* Set during the Christmas season, these stories tell about a school with great teachers and neat kids.

I'd like _____ copies of *All Eyes Up Here!* @ $14.95

I'd like _____ copies of *How Come the Wise Men Are In The DEMPSTER DUMPSTER®?* @ $10.95

Shipping & Handling $2 for first book, $1.50 for additional copies.

My check or money order (payable to CARR Enterprises) for $_____ is enclosed.

Please print:

Name: _____

Address: _____

City/State/Zip: _____

Telephone Area Code/Number: _____

Purchase Orders welcome.

Quantity Discounts Available

For educational or quantity discounts, call 423-698-5685 or FAX 423-698-3182.

CARR Enterprises
3 Belvoir Circle
Chattanooga, TN 37412

E-Mail: drtcarr@aol.com